Lord Jesus, Teach Me To Pray

A Seven Week Course in Personal Prayer

Lucy Rooney, S.N.D.
Robert Faricy, S.J.

Queenship
Publishing Company
P.O. Box 42028
Santa Barbara, CA 93140-2028
Phone (800) 647-9882 Fax (805)569-3274

Cover photograph by Marne Breckensiek, O.F.M.

Library of Congress #95-68113

ISBN #1-882972-55-4

Published by:
    Queenship Publishing
    P.O. Box 42028
    Santa Barbara, CA 93140-2028
    Phone (800) 647-9882 Fax (805)569-3274

Printed in the United States of America

Contents

Preface

Welcome to the twentieth century, the age running. We type this on a computer that is advertised as faster than its competitors and has to wait for our thinking to catch up. Yesterday we visited the Strategic Air Command Museum and saw intercontinental missiles that allow the enemy only eight minutes to react to a nuclear attack. We arrived at the museum via a highway where we can once again travel 65 m.p.h. and find fast food along the way prepared in one minute to taste like cardboard. We passed homes where latch-key children are waiting and wondering when their rushing parents will come home. . . or parent, since in our rushing and impersonal culture, half of all marriages end in divorce. And we passed joggers running along the highway. Nowadays we run even to relax.

But the faster people run, the more they hunger for moments of peace that rebuild the inner spirit. Each year our national parks host more visitors taking time to contemplate a sunset from a mountain ridge. Airlines have to offer free trips to a lazy Hawaiian beach to lure their fast-paced frequent fliers. Even retreat houses are bulging and need rubber walls to accommodate all those longing for a quiet weekend of prayer.

This book is for the person who hungers to meet God in peaceful silence. Its great strength is that Sr. Lucy Rooney and Fr. Robert Faricy have distilled four centuries of retreat experience based on *The Spiritual Exercises* of St. Ignatius into simple steps that help the beginner grow in loving and being loved by God. It answers basic questions: How do I begin to pray? How can I hear a "silent" God? How do I know I am hearing God when I make a decision? What do I do when I can't pray? How can the hurts I have suffered be healed?

To help us experience the answers to these questions and to gradually "look the Lord in the eye," the authors suggest a seven-week prayer experience, with a different way to pray each day. Each of the fortynine ways of praying suggested here takes only a few minutes a day, but yields peace and meaning for a lifetime—and an eternity.

Fr. Matthew Linn, S.J.
Sheila Fabricant, M.Div.
Fr. Dennis Linn, S.J.

For Diana Villegas

Come, let us go up to the mountain of the Lord,
 to the house of the God of Jacob;
that he may teach us his ways
 and we may walk in his paths.

(Micha 4:2)

Lord, teach us to pray.

(Luke 11:1)

How To Use This Manual

This book is a manual for a course on personal prayer. Jesus is the teacher. You are the learner. The course has as its purpose to help you in your personal prayer. It is designed especially, but not only, for people who have had at least some experience in charismatic renewal.

By "personal prayer," here we mean prayer alone with the Lord, quiet time with God, so-called "private prayer." All kinds of prayer, of course, have importance: praying with others, in the family, in a small or a larger prayer group, devotions in church, and of course worshiping God in church, especially in the Mass, are all important. But for all of these, personal prayer stands as the foundation. This course tries to help you in your personal prayer. And so, indirectly, it should help you in other kinds of prayer.

The course contains teachings on practical ways to pray, and it includes experiences that put into effect and reinforce these practical ways of praying. It does not take up the theory of prayer, what prayer is. Rather, it tries to teach how to pray, how to relate to God in prayer.

We have written the manual for one person. However, two or more persons can follow the course at the same time, perhaps meeting and sharing once or twice a week.

Course Structure.

The course lasts seven weeks. It consists of one reading each week plus (and this has maximum importance) the daily practice of personal prayer, based on assigned scripture texts. The daily prayer during the week is the most important part of the course. It is not absolutely necessary to use the scripture texts given in this book. It might be better in some cases to use the gospel readings of the liturgical season.

Course Content.

Each lesson has a reading, and points for daily prayer. The real course content is a process: the process of being in relation to the Lord in prayer. All the readings and all the prayer points feed into the process of personal prayer; they feed into personal relationship with the Lord in prayer.

We have deliberately omitted from the course any exercises or projects or programs that do not directly help to pray, to be with the Lord in prayer. Other books have interesting meditation exercises and engrossing projects that lead the reader to appreciate prayer or to understand prayer, or to love prayer. Our purpose here is none of these. It is simply to pray. The whole course and everything in it aim at teaching directly how to pray, how to go straight to the Lord in prayer. Everything in the course feeds directly into that one process: prayerful union with the Lord.

WEEK ONE:

Personal Prayer and the Lord's Love

The aim of the FIRST WEEK is to lay a solid foundation for the rest of the course by preparing you to pray faithfully and well during the first seven days of the prayer course. The first lesson tries to accomplish this aim by leading you to understand what you have to do to have a personal prayer life and by showing you the Lord's love for you, a love that calls you to prayer as a response to that love.

Course Teacher.

This book is a manual, but a manual is no use without a teacher. The Teacher in this prayer course is Jesus. "They shall all be taught by God" (John 6:45). "Lord, teach us to pray" (Luke 11:1)

Time Needed for the Course.

The prayer course takes six weeks to complete. You will need up to thirty or forty-five minutes once a week to go over the weekly lesson slowly. Try to do this on the same day every week, on Sunday for example.

And you will need a fixed, regular time every day for your personal prayer. This might be a time of twenty minutes, or thirty minutes, or an hour.

1

READING ON PRAYER

a. The Conditions of Prayer

What are the conditions for prayer? Not for "saying prayers," but for growing in a personal relationship with the Lord? What do I have to do to have personal prayer life?

On my side there are just two conditions: fidelity and openness.

Fidelity is spending time with the Lord regularly. I put time and effort into anything that is important to me. No relationship of love endures and grows unless time is spent together.

But the Lord is not a time-keeper. It is not the time itself that matters, but fidelity to the time spent with him. This is the measure of the quality of my commitment.

One cannot be fickle in friendship. That is what the Lord offers me. He said, "I no longer speak of you as slave—instead, I call you friends" (John 15:15). The Lord is always present with me. I need to turn to him, to be faithful in meeting him each day. The first step to that is putting in time. Then I am saying to him: "You are important to me. My relationship to you is the most important thing in my life (and is the foundation of all my other relationships). I might have to miss a meal to come to our meeting—but being with you means more to me that eating or sleeping. I want to put nothing in your place, nor ahead of you in my heart."

Openness. So I come faithfully to meet the Lord. What do I do then? I am open, attentive to him—just being there with him, looking at him in love, knowing in my heart what his attitude to me is.

I am needy and poor; but I do not always have to pray out of my neediness, out of my sinfulness and suffering. He knows all that. There are times in prayer for crying out to the Lord. But what pleases him is that I am there just for love of him. His love and presence are never static, but flowing; he will see and minister to my sin, my sickness. I can forget myself and love him. I can love myself too, despite what I see, because he, Jesus, loves me as he sees me to be—and he can't be wrong. So I become like a loving child. Jesus diagnoses my sickness—it makes him love me with even more compassion, as one loves a child, and loves it even more if possible because it is ill or defective. Jesus puts his arms around me, and I love him back with, maybe little, love—it doesn't matter. I rest quietly, loved and loving. "Whoever does not receive the kingdom of God like a child shall not enter it."

b. The Lord's Love Calls Me To Respond in Prayer

When I come into the presence of God he speaks my name in love. This is a great mystery—that I can actually enter into an intimate, loving, conscious relationship with God. It is above all a mystery of God's love for me.

I need to take seriously this love of God for me: the love of the Father who called me personally, lovingly into existence; the love of Jesus who in his saving love for me became man, lived, died, rose to life; the love of the Holy Spirit who lovingly works every moment in guiding and enabling me, bringing me to "the glory, as yet unrevealed, which is waiting for us" (Romans 8:18).

This love calls forth a response of love. I can accept the love of each divine person, and respond in love, praise, thanksgiving. My response to God is prayer. Prayer is not just reading and thinking. It is a reaching out to God—a movement of my heart, a lifting of heart and mind to him.

Prayer doesn't always need words. Love doesn't always need to be felt. My fidelity in coming to meet the Lord is love; my staying to the end of our time together is love. The love is mainly on God's side—my love is always a poor thing but the best I have and therefore precious in his sight. In fact, the only thing the Lord needs from me is my personal love for him. He has everything else: "If I were hungry, I should not tell you, since the world and all it holds is mine" (Psalm 50:12).

The mystery of God, and the mystery that this God loves me and wants, needs, my love can overwhelm my mind—I cannot encompass this with my mind. This is the time just to be there, simply, looking at God with what little love I have, blind, but seeing.

c. The Grace I Want from the Lord This Week:

To know him better as loving me and as calling me to love him back by being present to him faithfully in my prayer every day this coming week. My whole prayer on a given day, or even all seven days, should take the form of simply asking the Lord for this grace.

In my prayer, I can use the gospel reference in any way that helps me to relate to the Lord. The way that will best suit most persons is not to think about the scripture, not to reflect quietly on its meaning or its significance, but rather to use it as a means, a starting point or a kind of framework, for looking at Jesus, accepting his love, loving him back. The best prayer ordinarily is not thinking but contemplating.

d. When Should I Pray?

Whenever suits my personal schedule and temperament: early in the morning, mid-day lunch break, before supper, late at night. Whenever I can pray and have most peace.

I should have a fixed, regular time for my personal prayer. I should try to pray every day at the same time. If for some reason I miss my time for prayer, then I should try hard to make it up later.

How Long Should I Pray? I should have for my personal prayer a certain minimum amount of time every day. How long a time depends how the Lord leads me. Each person has to decide: How long do I think the Lord is calling me to spend every day in my personal prayer? Perhaps an hour.

Perhaps thirty minutes. Perhaps twenty minutes. Perhaps I should begin with twenty minutes and then, during the six weeks of this course, gradually build up to a longer time.

What Bodily Position Should I Use? Sitting, kneeling, prostrating, cross-legged—any reverent bodily position.

Where Should I Pray? A church is a specially graced place to pray. But anywhere where I can be alone and undisturbed—wherever I can best meet the Lord—is the best place. It might be my room or a corner of my home, or it might be out of doors. If I pray in my room or my home, I might want to light a candle, or use an icon or picture or statue to set an atmosphere and help me focus my attention on the Lord.

DAILY PRAYER FOR WEEK ONE:

Entering into the Love of the Lord

Week One, Day One:

1. Read John 15:1-10

2. Ask Jesus for the grace that I want: to know him better as loving me, and as calling me to respond to his love in my prayer.

3. Points to help in contemplating Jesus:
(i) "Abide in me, and I in you. . . .I am the vine, you are the branches" (verses 4-5).
(ii) "As the Father loves me, so I love you; continue in my love" (verse 9).
(iii) "If you abide in me, and my words abide in you, then you ask for whatever you want, and it will be done" (verse 7).

4. Prayer that may be said slowly at the beginning of the prayer time, or at the end, or from time to time during the prayer time, or as part of morning or night prayers:
Lord Jesus,
thank you for loving me so much.
Thank you for being a friend who loves me enough
that you laid down your life for me.
Help me to take you seriously as loving me.
Thank you for loving me
and for taking me seriously.
Jesus, I love you.
Teach me to know you better as loving me.
Amen.

5. A phrase to plant in your heart for the day. You might want to repeat it from time to time: "Thank you, Lord, for loving me," Or: "I love you, Lord." Or: "Abide in me, and I in you."

Week One, Day Two:

1. Read John 15:11-17.

2. Ask Jesus for the grace that I want: to know you, better, Jesus, as loving me, and as calling me to respond to your love in my prayer today and every day.

3. Points to help in contemplating Jesus:
    (i) "Greater love than this no one has, that a man lay down his life for his friends" (verse 13).
    (ii) "Your are my friends" (verse 14).
    (iii) " You have not chosen me; I have chosen you" (verse 16).

4. Prayer to be said slowly during your quiet time with the Lord, and/or as part of morning and/or night prayers:
    Lord Jesus,
    thank you for your loving friendship.
    Help me to know you better as my friend
    who loves me enough to have died for me.
    I want to love you more,
    and to be a better friend to you.
    Jesus, I love you.
    Teach me to know you better
    as my loving friend.
    Amen.

5. To plant in your heart for the day; you might want to repeat it during the day from time to time: "Lord, you have

chosen me." Or: "I love you, Lord." Or: "Thank you, Lord, for loving me."

Week One, Day Three:

1. Read Jesus' prayer for you to the Father, especially: John 17:20-26.

2. Ask Jesus for the grace that I want: Lord Jesus, teach me to know you better as loving me with a personal love, and as calling me to respond to your love in my prayer.

3. Points to help in contemplating Jesus:
    (i) "Father! I pray that they may be in us, just as you are in me and I am in you" (verse 21).
    (ii) "I in them and you in me, so that they may be completely one, in order that the world might know that you sent me and that you love them as you love me" (verse 23).
    (iii) "I have made your name known to them, and I will keep on making it known to them so that the love that you love me with may be in them, and so I may be in them" (verse 26).

4. Prayer to say slowly during your prayer time, or in morning prayers or in night prayers, or all three:
    Jesus, I love you.
    Thank you for loving me
    and for living in me.
    Thank you because you pray
    for me to the Father.
    Thank you, Jesus, because
    the Father loves me in you,
    Jesus, and you in me.
    Help me to know you better as loving me.
    Amen.

5. To place in your heart, and perhaps to repeat during the day: "Jesus, help me to know you better." Or: "I love you, Lord." Or: "Thank you, Lord, for loving me." Or: "Praise you, Lord; your love is everlasting."

Week One, Day Four:

1. Read Jesus' teaching on love in Luke 6:32-38; in your prayer, apply this teaching of Jesus about how we should practice love to Jesus himself. How he teaches us to love is how he loves; he practices what he preaches. So the scripture passage here, although about how you should love, can be applied now by you to Jesus to see how he loves you.

2. Pray for the grace that you want Jesus to give you in your prayer:
Lord Jesus, help me to know you better
and to take you seriously in your love for me.
Teach me how you love me:
without judging me,
without condemning me,
but forgiving me, giving me yourself.

3. Points to help you to contemplate Jesus teaching the crowds about love (look at Jesus teaching about love, and know that what he is teaching about love is what he lived, lives now, is):
(i) "Judge not , and you will not be judged" (verse 37); Jesus does not judge me.
(ii) "Do not condemn, and you will not be condemned" (verse 27); Jesus does not condemn me.
(iii) "Forgive, and you will be forgiven; give and it will be given to you generously" (verses 37-38); Jesus forgives me, and he gives me his love generously.

4. A prayer to read slowly and prayerfully during your quiet time with the Lord and/or as part of your morning and night prayer:

> Jesus, you do not judge me.
> You do not condemn me.
> You forgive me.
> You give me your love.
> You give me your self.
> You accept me totally and unconditionally
> just as I am.
> Teach me to know your love
> and accept it,
> to know you and to open my heart
> to your love for me.
> Amen.

5. To place in your heart for short prayers during the day: "Jesus, reveal to me your love for me." Or: "Your love is everlasting" (refrain of Psalm 136).

Week One, Day Five:

1. Read Matthew 11:25-30.

2. Pray for the grace that you want from Jesus in this prayer time:

> Jesus, reveal to me yourself,
> your heart,
> your love for me,
> so that I can know you better.

3. Points to help to contemplate Jesus teaching about coming to him:

(i) "I thank you, Father; because you hide these things from the wise and prudent, and you reveal them to little children" (verse 25).

(ii) "Come to me, you who work hard and are heavily burdened, and I will give you rest" (verse 28).

(iii) "Learn from me: I am meek and lowly of heart; and you will find rest for your soul. My yoke is easy and my burden is light" (verses 29-30).

4. Here is a prayer you can say slowly during your prayer time and/or in morning and night prayers:

Jesus, thank you for inviting
me to come to you
and to learn from you,
to take your yoke upon me
and your burden which is the cross of my life.
I come to you to learn from you,
and to take your yoke
that unites me to you.
Your yoke is love.
Amen.

5. To plant in your heart for brief prayer throughout the day: "I come to you, Jesus." Or: "I want to learn from you; you are meek and lowly of heart." Or: "Thank you, Lord, for loving me."

Week One, Day Six:

1. Read Jesus' teaching on prayer in Luke 11:1-13.

2. Prayer for the grace I want:
    Lord Jesus,
    I want to know you better.
    Teach me to pray.

3. Points to help contemplate Jesus teaching you how to pray:
    (i) "Lord, teach us to pray" (verse 1).
    (ii) "Ask, and it will be given to you; seek, and you will find; knock, and it will be opened for you" (verse 9).
    (iii) "How much more will your Father in heaven give the Holy Spirit to those who ask him?" (verse 13).

4. A prayer to say slowly as part of your regular daily prayer, and/or in your morning and night prayer:
    Jesus, teach me to pray.
    In your love for me,
    teach me to come to you
    with childlike trust in you.
    Teach me to turn to the Father
    with childlike trust.
    Teach me to pray
    simply, without many words,
    with love,
    as a response to your love for me
    and to the Father's love for me.
    Amen.

5. To place in your heart for recalling during the day: "Lord, teach us (me) to pray" (verse 1). Or: "Lord, I love you; thank you for loving me.

Week One, Day Seven:

1. Read about Jesus and the little children, and Jesus' teaching on childlikeness in Mark 10:13-16.

2. Pray for the grace that you want:
Jesus, help me to know you
and to come to you
simply, like a little child.

3. Points to help you to contemplate Jesus welcoming, laying hands on, and blessing the little children:
(i) "Let the little children come to me" (verse 14).
(ii) "Whoever does not receive the kingdom of God like a little child will not enter it" (verse 15).
(iii) "He took them into his arms, laid his hands upon them, and blessed them" (verse 16).

4. Here is a prayer to say slowly during your prayer time and/or as part of your morning and evening prayer:
Lord Jesus, I want to come
to you like a little child.
Give me the grace of simplicity
in my relationship with you.
Take me into your arms.
Lay hands on me.
Bless me.
Amen.

5. To plant in your heart to repeat during the day: "Lay your hand gently upon me." Or: "Jesus, I trust in you."

WEEK TWO:

Removing Obstacles to Prayer:
Sin, Disordered Attachments, Distractions

The goal of the SECOND WEEK is twofold: (1) to go to the Lord asking him to remove whatever might be blocking me in prayer, to show me any disordered attachments, and to help me order my life; and (2) to prepare me for daily prayer during the second week, during which I ask for these same graces.

READING ON SIN, ATTACHMENTS, AND DISTRACTIONS

a. Sin and Forgiveness

The prayer this week is not an examination of conscience. Rather, I come to Jesus, and, looking at him, know that I am greatly loved and forgiven.

I know from bitter experience that what the psalmist says is true: "I was born guilty, a sinner from the moment of conception" (Psalm 51:5). We sin many times. This is a reality, my reality. I know I am weak and fickle. This draws the heart of Jesus to me because he is all compassion and love. His name is Jesus, which means Savior. I need him to save me. So I come, looking at him, not at my sin. I ask Jesus to look at my sin and to show me where sin is in my life. He will show me, not out of condemnation, but out of his love for me. My sinfulness is real. It crucified him. Now, coming to know him in love, I can face the wrong things in my life, and I can see things to which, until now, I have been blind. It is essential to be honest and realistic as far as I can.

After facing up to what the Lord shows me, I acknowledge my sin and I pray, asking for repentance, that is, for the grace to be so sorry that I want to change. It really is Jesus' forgiving love that moves me to repent. So I ask Jesus, I ask the Father, to forgive me.

The prodigal son (Luke 15:11-32) was not really repentant when he returned home. He was merely miserable about his state. He intended (though he did not realize it) to bargain with his father: "Make me one of your hired men" (verse 20). He was saying, "I will earn forgiveness from you." But when his father, seeing his son a long way off, ran to meet him and took him in his arms, then the boy forgot his speech about being a hired servant. He was bathed, dressed, and restored to his dignity as a son solely out of his father's forgiving love. Then he really repented: "I am not worthy to be called your son" (verse 22).

So, in our sinfulness, we must not wait until we are perfect before coming to Jesus. Give yourself to him now as you are. He wants you, needs you, now.

b. Identifying and Straightening Our Disordered Attachments

In prayer I am telling Jesus that he is the chief person in my life, that all my other loves are vivified by that central love, that all my other relationships are founded on my relationship with him.

Does loving Jesus mean being detached form everything else? No. The Lord wants me to be deeply attached to those whom he has given me to love. He wants me to be attached to my work, to places, to things. I cannot have too much love in my life. But attachment, love, can be disordered.

Outright wrong attachments are easily seen. They lead me away from the Lord. But others, good ones, tend to get out of hand, to be disordered. They distract me from the Lord.

c. Distractions in Prayer

Thoughts that come to me in prayer—thoughts of people, events, worries—do not have to be distractions. I can just lift up the person and/or situation, momentarily, to the Lord, putting them in his hands. Then I resume my simple looking-with-love at Jesus. There may be need to pray specifically about these things at another time, but not now, during my quiet time with the Lord.

If the thoughts keep returning, it may be a lure of the devil to distract me, or it may be just my struggle to keep this attachment where it belongs as secondary to my attachment to the Lord. So, I just again and again, very briefly, even wordlessly, hold up whomever or whatever it is. In that way, I and they profit, Jesus is honored, and the devil is defeated.

But thoughts which really interfere and take over my time of prayer, thoughts which come between me and the Lord, are clues to disordered attachments. I need to pray, asking Jesus for light, to see these disordered attachments, and asking that I may bring them under his lordship. My personal relationship to Jesus is central. Whatever is an obstacle to that union is disordered.

If the disordered attachment is to a friend, I need to ask the Lord to teach me to love as he does, with interior freedom, not possessively, leaving my friend free, not manipulating or using that person for self-gratification.

If the distraction is obsession with a problem I ask the grace of trust. I realize that my problems are Jesus' problems, because he is my Friend and my Lord. I need to put them trustfully in his hands, asking his guidance, his solution.

17

The nature of love is to want to love and be loved with a freely given, undivided love. Jesus is vulnerable in love. He wants my whole heart and offers me his, but he leaves me free.

d. Some Practical Points for the Coming Week's Daily Prayer

(i) Stay where you find fruit. The point of your prayer is to be close to Jesus. So go slowly, and stay where you find Jesus.

(ii) Let Jesus reveal your sinfulness to you. You do not have to make any examination of conscience this week in your prayer. Let *the Lord* show you your sinfulness.

(iii) Sentiments and the heart count for more than words, ideas, or thinking.

DAILY PRAYER FOR WEEK TWO:

Repentance and Accepting
the Lord's Forgiveness

Week Two, Day One:

1. Read the account of Jesus healing the blind man: Luke 18:35-43.

2. Ask Jesus for the grace that I want: to know Jesus better as loving me and revealing to me my sinfulness, and that I am a sinner whom he forgives; to know Jesus better so that the light of love can better reveal my sinfulness before him; to know Jesus and his love for me better so that I can therefore repent more sincerely of my sins.

3. Points to help in contemplating Jesus:
   (i) And he cried out, "Jesus, son of David, have mercy on me" (verse 38).
   (ii) "Lord, That I may see" (verse 41).
   (iii) "Receive your sight; your faith has saved you" (verse 42).

4. A prayer you can say slowly during your prayer time and / or as part of you morning and evening prayer:
   Lord Jesus, thank you for loving me
   and for accepting me totally,
   without qualifications, just as I am.
   Jesus, I can be blind to my sins,
   to my sinfulness before you.
   Lead me into the light of your love for me
   so that I may see—

so that I may see you loving me,
and so that I may see my own sinfulness
more clearly in the light of your love.
Lord, that I may see.
Amen.

5. To plant in your heart to repeat during the day: "Lord, that I may see." Or: "Jesus, have mercy on me."

Week Two, Day Two:

1. Read the account of Jesus forgiving and healing the paralytic: Matthew 9:1-18.

2. The grace that I want:
    Jesus, help me to know
    you better as loving me,
    as looking on my helplessness and weakness
    and sinfulness with great compassion;
    I want to accept your
    forgiveness and healing.

3. Points to help me contemplate Jesus:
    (i) "Be happy; your sins are forgiven" (verse 2).
    (ii) "Which is easier to say: 'Your sins are forgiven,' or 'Arise and walk'?" (verse 5).
    (iii) "The Son of Man has power on earth to forgive sins" (verse 6).

4. A prayer to say slowly during your prayer time and/or as part of morning and night prayers:
    Jesus, thank you for forgiving me my sins.
    Heal me with your forgiveness.

Heal the roots of sin in me.
Lay your hands gently upon me.
Let them bring your forgiveness and healing.
Amen.

5. To place in your heart for recall during the day: "Hear, O Lord, and have mercy on me" (Psalm 30:10). Or: "Your mercy endures forever" (see Psalm 107:1). Or: "Lay your hands gently upon me."

Week Two, Day Three:

1. Read about Jesus healing a leper: Matthew 8:1-4.

2. Pray for the grace that you want:
    Lord Jesus, I want to know you better
    as healing my heart and my soul
    through your loving compassion for me.

3. Points to help in contemplating Jesus:
    (i) "Lord, if you will, you can make me clean" (verse 2).
    (ii) "I will; be clean" (verse 3).
    (iii) "Go on your way, and show yourself to the priest" (verse 4).
    Note: Week Two is a good time to go to confession. If the Lord so leads you, you could even make a general confession of your whole life.

4. Prayer for use during your quiet time with the Lord and/or during morning and night prayer:
    Lord Jesus, your mercy makes me whole.
    Your forgiveness washes me clean.
    Thank you for loving me so much

that you forgive me
and make me whole and strong against sin.
Let me walk always in your loving mercy.
Amen.

5. To plant in your heart, to repeat throughout the day: "Lord, if you will, you can make me clean." Or: "Lay your hands gently upon me."

Week Two, Day Four:

1. Read Jesus' teaching on forgiveness in Matthew 6:12-15.

2. Pray to know Jesus better:
    Jesus, teach me to know you better
    in your wanting to forgive me.
    And show me whom I should forgive
    so that I can better receive your forgiveness
    and the forgiveness of the Father.
    Help me to forgive now those
    who have hurt me.

3. Points to help me to contemplate Jesus:
    (i) "Forgive us our trespasses as we forgive those who trespass against us" (verse 12).
    (ii) "If you forgive others, your Father in heaven will forgive you" (verse 14).
    (iii) "If you do not forgive them, he will not forgive you" (verse 15).

4. Prayer to say slowly during your prayer time and/or in morning and night prayer:
    Jesus, open my heart completely
    to receive your forgiveness.

Give me an open heart,
open to your loving compassion,
and open to others in forgiveness,
especially to those who have hurt me.
Lord Jesus,
show me who has hurt me in my life:
my father, my mother, my husband or wife,
teachers, priests, nuns, brothers or sisters.
I forgive each one.
Heal the hurts each has caused me.
And, Jesus, I accept your forgiveness,
and the Father's forgiveness
that you bring me.
Amen.

5. To place in your heart to recall during the day: "Lay your hands gently upon me." Or: "Forgive us our trespasses as we forgive those who trespass against us."

Week Two, Day Five:

1. Read the story of Zacchaeus, Luke 19:1-10, and the Mary Magdalene story in Luke 7:36-50. Choose the passage that you can identify with.

2. Prayer for the grace that I want:
    Jesus, help me to know you better
    as calling me to receive your healing
    and transforming forgiveness.

3. Points to help in contemplating Jesus:
    (i) "Zacchaeus was rich . . . he could not see Jesus because he was small of stature" (Luke 19:2-3). Or: "A woman who was a sinner . . . brought an alabaster jar full of per-

fumed ointment and stood at his feet" (Luke 7:37-38).

(ii) "Zacchaeus, come down; today I come to your house" (Luke 19:5). Or: "She has washed my feet with tears . . . has kissed my feet . . . has anointed my feet with ointment; her sins, which are many, are forgiven because she has loved much—those who are forgiven little, love little" (Luke 7:44-47).

(iii) "The Son of Man has come to seek and to save the lost" (Luke 19:10). Or: "Your faith has save you; go in peace" (Luke 7:50).

4. Prayer to say slowly during your prayer time and/or during morning and night prayer:

Jesus, show me what I need
to correct in my life.
Reveal to me my selfishness, my self-seeking.
Show me where I am possessive.
Reveal to me where my
attachments are disordered,
not according to what you want,
not straight and in your Spirit.
Help me to renounce my possessiveness,
my self-seeking,
and whatever is not from you.
Help me, Jesus.
Amen.

5. Phrases you can put in your heart to recall during the day: "Jesus, help me to order my life according to your will." Or: "Your will be done." Or simply recall an image or picture during the day: Zacchaeus in the tree and Jesus calling him; or the sinful woman washing and anointing Jesus' feet.

Week Two, Day Six:

1. Read the story of the prodigal son: Luke 15:11-32.

2. Pray for the grace that you want from Jesus:
   Lord Jesus,
   help me to know you better
   as the kind of person who tells me this story
   about the Father's merciful love
   and about your merciful love.

3. Points to help in contemplating Jesus telling you this story:
   (i) "I have sinned against heaven and against you"
   (verse 18).
   (ii) " When he was yet a great way off, his father saw him
   and had compassion for him, and ran and hugged him
   and kissed him" (verse 20).
   (iii) "You are always with me, and all that I have is yours
   . . . but your brother was dead and is now alive, was lost
   and has been found" (verses 31-31).

4. Here is a prayer to say slowly during your quiet time with
the Lord, and/or during morning and night prayer:
   Lord Jesus, thank you for this story
   about the Father's merciful and
   forgiving love for me,
   and about your merciful and
   forgiving love for me.
   I see you, Jesus, on the road ahead of me.
   I am like the younger son,
   you are like the father in the story.
   I walk into your arms
   and your embrace restores my lost dignity;
   it renews me in my relationship with you.

You are glad, joyful, that I come to you.
Thank you, Jesus.
Amen.

5. To place in your heart, to repeat prayerfully during the day: "Although I walk in the midst of trouble, you will give me new life" (Psalm 138:7). Or: "Thank you, Lord, for loving me."

Week Two, Day Seven:

1. Read Matthew 9:9-13.

2. Pray for the grace that you want the Lord to give you in this time with him:
     Jesus, give me the grace to know you better
     as forgiving my sins
     and as calling me to yourself.

3. Points to help in contemplating Jesus:
     (i) "He saw a man named Matthew . . . and he said to him, 'Follow me.' And he rose and followed Jesus" (verse 9).
     (ii) "It is not those who are healthy who need a doctor, but those who are ill" (verse 12).
     (iii) "Learn what this means: I want mercy and not sacrifice; I have come to call not the righteous but sinners to repentance" (verse 13).

4. A prayer to read and pray slowly during your prayer time and/or during morning and night prayer:
     Lord Jesus, you have shown me my sinfulness.
     You forgive me and renew me.
     And you call me, a forgiven sinner,

to follow you.
You love me and call me,
partly because I am a sinner.
My need for you makes me
more attractive to you.
My sinfulness calls out to
your forgiving love.
So I will glory in my infirmities
because the power of your love
is made perfect in my weakness.
Amen.

5. To plant in your heart for prayerful recall during the day:
"Jesus, you have come to call sinners." Or: "Heal me, Jesus."

WEEK THREE:

Inner Healing

The THIRD WEEK builds on the first and second lessons and on the daily prayer of the first and second weeks. This third lesson has a twofold purpose: (1) to pray for and to receive inner healing; and (2) to prepare for the coming week's daily prayer in which we continue to pray for and to receive the inner healing the Lord wants to give us, and in which we listen to the Lord's call to be with him, and respond wholeheartedly to that call.

READING AND PRAYER: INNER HEALING

a. What Is Inner Healing?
    It includes spiritual healing and emotional healing.
    (i) Spiritual healing means the forgiveness of sins and the strength and interior wholeness that come from accepting the Lord's forgiveness.
    (ii) Emotional healing means the healing of hurtful feelings that in some cases could act as the roots of sinful tendencies. One way of praying for emotional healing is to pray for healing of memories.
    (iii) Healing of memories means that the Lord heals my hurtful memories, my memories of painful and humiliating

times in my life. The Lord does not cause me to forget past hurts, but he does take the hurt out of the memory of what happened. And so he changes the meaning and effect of that memory. I do not forget, but now—because Jesus has healed me—I can praise him for all that happened, even for the worst things, because I know that he has written my life straight even though with crooked lines. He allowed these hurts so that I could grow through them and so that he could heal me of them.

Some painful memories are subject to conscious recall. But many lie buried in my unconscious. I cannot remember what happened. Perhaps those hurts happened to me when I was quite a small infant, or during birth, or before my birth. Jesus sees those buried memories, and he can heal them.

Some hurtful memories are conscious—of an overly possessive mother, of a too strict father, of an alcoholic in the family, of suffering in school, of consequences of my own sinful actions. The Lord wants to heal those memories. I can simply hand them over to him. I can let Jesus come into those memories, taking out of them my anger or depression or rebelliousness or humiliation or discouragement or fear, filling those memories with his loving and healing presence.

b. Prayer for Healing of Memories

Here is a prayer to read over slowly and prayerfully now. Stop wherever you think the Lord might be healing you. Wait. Then go on. And Add on to the prayer in your own words, asking the Lord to heal particular memories.

From Conception to Birth: Come, Lord Jesus! Take me by the hand and walk with me through my life from the very moment of my conception.

You were there, Lord, in that moment. If there was anything wrong genetically, or anything that would damage me psychologically, heal me now. You were there while I was being formed in my mother's womb. You can see the things that are still within me, buried in my subconscious, the suffering which has remained beneath the levels of conscious memory: what I suffered for lack of space, the difficulty I had in being nourished or in assimilating nourishment, the smoking or drinking my mother did not have the courage to give up, her precarious health or psychological traumas, her tension or worries, my having been conceived in an unsuitable moment, maybe outside matrimony. You can see where I need healing. Pour out your love and your compassion like water that gives life and leads to flowering. Let it flow over me and penetrate into me like a sponge. I do not know what you are going to heal in me; I just want to absorb every drop of your healing love.

Childhood: I cannot remember anything about my birth, Lord, but I know I suffered, that it was difficult for me. All that light, the noise, the strangers, the cold hostile world. Heal these buried memories. Let me hear your reassuring voice calling me to life, calling me by name. Take that little child I was in your hands, hold me up to your cheek and tightly to you so that I can hear the beating of your heart. Comfort and console me, give me the love that you desire so that I may be filled with your love.

And if my mother could not feed me and had to have recourse to artificial means, lay me on Mary's breast so that my little hands can reach out for the contact, the warmth and the security I need and my eyes can encounter the smile on her face.

I can see you, Lord, at home where I used to sleep and eat and play. Everything is bathed in your presence. You are looking at the child that I was. Moments of solitude, of sadness, of misunderstanding and of fear . . . Heal me, Lord, from all the hurts inflicted on me during the first few years of my life.

Even if I have him no longer, I remember my father as I

saw him then, I thank and praise you for his goodness, for everything he did and underwent for me. But he was not perfect. I want to forgive him now, in your presence, for the times he humiliated me and made me feel unwanted or inadequate, for the times he caused me suffering because of his absence, his misunderstanding and severity, or by ill-treating my mother or my brothers and sisters.

In my imagination, I move toward him and hug him, saying: "I forgive you!" . . . Unite us, Lord, in your Spirit of love and forgiveness. Heal our relationship.

Jesus, I can see myself with my mother, and you are with us. Heal whatever may have been difficult or wrong in our relationship. She, too, had her own defects and faults, some of which caused me a lot of suffering: disinterest, impatience, anxiety, complexes and things she would not talk about, jealousy, preferences, hopes and expectations I could not live up to . . . With you, Jesus, I embrace her. Thank you for her presence in my life. Thank you for having chosen her for me. I thank her, too, and forgive her, and if she is already with you in paradise I ask her to pray for my healing.

Help me, Lord, to remember in you all the unhappy moments of my childhood, I offer you everything you want to heal. When I was little it was difficult and often painful for me to socialize with other children, and the first occasions I was without my mother and the family hurt me deeply. The others were often hard and relentless with me or they undermined my self-confidence, making fun of me because of my weight or height, slowness, or lack of intelligence and vivacity. And school, Lord, was often a torment for me, with the teacher who did not understand me of who humiliated me, the subjects I could not fathom, and the bad marks which, in spite of all I tried to do, always disappointed my parents' ambitions. But you, Lord, loved me just the same, with my failures, my capriciousness and my talking back, and now you want to heal those hurts and remove all those things which are rooted in my painful memories and constitute an obstacle between you and me, and between myself and others.

Heal me, Lord Jesus, and I shall be healed!

Adolescence: I offer you the first ten years of my life, Lord, so that you may heal them. Then puberty: it was a very delicate time for me. Take me by the hand now, Lord, as you did then, and walk together with me through these difficult years.

I understood almost nothing of the rapid changes in my body and in my emotions, In any case, little or nothing had been explained to me because adults were inhibited then, and unable to see it all as an immense gift from you. I was often ungainly or unpleasant, stupid or impertinent without knowing why. But you, Lord, understood me with all my difficulties and humiliations, my ignorance and even my sin; you understood me then as you do now.

You have mercy on the mess you can see, and you forgive me. You forgive me the things that I should not have read and the bad friendships; you forgive what adults may have done to me while I was an adolescent. You feel for the solitude they left me in, just as you do for the memory of having been used by them which is still alive in me. Heal me from my fears, from the memory of the sins of my adolescence, from the many times I was a failure, from all the wounds inside me that go back to that time.

Adulthood : Heal me, Lord, now in my present state of life. Heal each on of my close relationships.

Conclusion: I am not asking you, Lord, that I be able to forget all these things. I do not want to forget anything. I only want you to take away from these negative memories all the suffering and pain, all the humiliation, all the shame and resentment, so that I can praise you, Lord, for the sufferings and difficulties and mixed up things in my life. I have not always been faithful, Lord: I have sinned and you know it. Forgive me and heal me from the consequences of my unfaithfulness. I have been unfaithful in prayer, in my interpersonal relationships, in carrying out my duties. But I have not left you, Lord, nor have you abandoned me. Have mercy on me, unfaithful by nature, lacking in love, weak and needy. Heal the roots of my unfaithfulness. Give me the gift of a new freedom. Free me, Lord, from sin, above all from not loving enough, from loving badly: gratifying my own needs but using other people, sometimes even in the name of love.

You know me, Lord, through and through, and you understand me fully. I do not know or understand myself: I do what I do not understand myself; I do what I do not want to do, say what I do not think, and am what I never supposed I was. Heal me, Lord, and I shall be healed!

c. Preparation for the Week's Daily Prayer

For at least a few days, the daily prayer takes the form of prayer for inner healing. If painful memories or negative emotions connected with past hurts come to the surface today or during the week, this is a sign that the Lord wants to continue to heal those memories, those emotions, those hurts. How to handle those disturbing images or thoughts or feelings tied to past hurts? I give them explicitly to Jesus so that He can heal me, so that he can change the meaning of my memories by healing the hurts in them. Certainly I do not dig around in my memory for past hurts. But if something comes to the surface, I give it to the Lord.

An important principle: Stay where you find fruit. If your prayer is fruitful, unites you more closely with the Lord, stay right there; do not change your prayer as long as you find it fruitful. Monday's and Tuesday's points for prayer concern inner healing. The rest of the week's prayer takes the shape of saying "Yes" to the Lord and of getting to know him better. But you may find that you want to remain with the theme of inner healing. You may find that the Lord wants to continue to heal you in and through your prayer. If so, stay there. Either adapt the prayer to fit your need, inner healing, or remain with Monday's and Tuesdays's points, or make your own points for prayer to suit that way you feel the Lord is leading you. Do not try to go faster than the Lord seems to lead you. Stay where you find fruit.

DAILY PRAYER FOR WEEK THREE:

Inner Healing;
Responding to Jesus' Call

Week Three, Day One:

1. Read Luke 4:38-42.

2. Ask Jesus for the grace that I want: to receive his healing and compassionate love and to be healed in my inner self.

3. Points to help you to contemplate Jesus and to receive his healing love:
    (i) "And he stood over her and rebuked the fever, and it left her" (verse 38).
    (ii) "And he laid his hands on every one of them and healed them" (verse 40).
    (iii) "And the people sought him and came to him" (verse 42).

4. Here is a prayer to say slowly during your prayer time and/or as a part of your morning and evening prayer:
    Lord Jesus, heal me.
    Heal in me whatever
    you see needs healing.
    Heal me of whatever might
    separate me from you.
    Heal my memory.
    Heal my heart.
    Heal my emotions.
    Heal my spirit.
    Lay your hands gently upon me.
    And heal me through your love for me.
    Amen.

5. To put in your heart to repeat during the day: "Heal me, Jesus." Or: "Lay your hands gently upon me."

Week Three, Day Two:

1. Read Luke 5:15-26.

2. I ask the Lord for the grace that I want: to receive his healing and compassionate love, and to be healed where Jesus sees I need healing.

3. Points to help contemplate Jesus and to receive his healing love:
    (i) "Great multitudes gathered to hear and to be healed of their infirmities" (verse 15).
    (ii) " Your sins are forgiven you" (verse 20).
    (iii) "He said to the man who was paralyzed, 'I say to you, rise, take up your bed and go home'" (verse 24).

4. Prayer:
    Lord Jesus, heal me.
    Thank you for forgiving all my sins.
    Heal me, Jesus, at the roots of my sins.
    Heal me interiorly so that
    I can come closer to you.
    Heal my heart, my mind, my soul, my body.
    Come, Lord Jesus.
    Amen.

5. To place in your heart to recall during the day: "Heal me, Jesus." Or: "Lay your hands gently upon me."

Week Three, Day Three:

1. Read Luke 5:1-11, the call of the first disciples.

2. I ask Jesus for the grace that I want:
   Jesus, Help me to hear you
   calling me by name to follow you,
   and to answer that call generously.

3. Points to help to contemplate Jesus calling me to follow him:
   (i) "Simon Peter fell down at Jesus' knees saying, 'Depart from me, for I am a sinful man, O Lord.' For he was astonished, and all that were with him, at the catch of fish which they had taken. And so also were James and John, sons of Zebedee, who were partners with Simon" (verses 8-10).
   (ii) "And Jesus said to Simon, 'Do not be afraid, henceforth you will be catching men'" (verse 10).
   (iii) "And when they had brought their boats to land, they left everything and followed him" (verse 11).

4. Prayer:
   Lord Jesus, you call me by name
   to follow you.
   Help me to listen to you,
   to hear you,
   to leave anything and everything
   that keeps me from you,
   to follow you in faith and in love.
   Amen.

5. To recall during the day: "Yes, Jesus." Or: "Thank you, Jesus, for calling me."

Week Three, Day Four:

1. Read Luke 5:27-32; Jesus calls Levi to follow him.

2. Ask Jesus for the grace that you want: to respond whole-heartedly to his calling me. Jesus calls me by name to follow him I want the grace to hear his call and to answer it generously.

3. Some points to help to contemplate Jesus inviting me to follow him, to be with him, to be his friend and companion and co-worker:

(i) "Jesus saw a tax collector, named Levi, sitting at the tax office, and he said to him, 'Follow me'" (verse 27).

(ii) "And he left everything, and rose and followed him" (verse 28).

(iii) "Jesus answered them, 'Those who are well have no need of a physician, but those who are sick. I have not come to call the righteous, but sinners to repentance'" (verses 31-32).

4. Prayer:

Jesus, help me to hear your call,
to listen to you calling me by name,
and to answer you,
to say, "Yes, Jesus."
Yes, Jesus,
I hear you,
and I want to follow you,
to be with you,
your friend,
your companion and co-worker.
Yes, Jesus.
Amen.

5. To recall during the day: "Yes, Jesus." Or: "Thank you, Jesus, for calling me."

Week Three, Day Five:

1. Read Luke 1:26-38, the Incarnation.

2. I ask Jesus for the grace that I want: to enter into the mystery of his becoming human to save me. I want to know him better so that I can love him more and follow him more closely. The fundamental grace that I want here, then, is to know Jesus better.

3. Points for contemplating the mystery of the Incarnation:

(i) "And the angel said to her, 'Do not be afraid, Mary, for you have found favor with God. And behold you will conceive in your womb and bear a son, and you shall call his name Jesus. He will be great, and will be called the Son of the Most High'" (verses 30-32).

(ii) "And the angel said to her, 'The Holy Spirit will come upon you and the power of the Most High will overshadow you; therefore the child to be born will be called holy, the Son of God'" (verse 35).

(iii) "And Mary said, 'Behold, I am the handmaid of the Lord; let it be done to me according to your word'" (verse 38).

Note: You may want to make this contemplation by praying to Mary first, that she lead you to Jesus. Or you may want to thank the Father for sending Jesus to be conceived in Mary. Pray the way the Spirit leads.

4. Prayer (in three parts):
(i) Mary, the Mother of Jesus, teach me to pray.
     Teach me to be open to the Holy Spirit.
     And lead me to Jesus.
     Pray with me now for
     the grace to know Jesus better
     so that I can love him more
     and follow him more closely.
(ii) Jesus, I come to you with your mother.
     Help me to know you better
     so that I can love you more
     and follow you more closely.
(iii) God my Father,
     thank you for sending your Son Jesus.
     Jesus is my way to you and
     my Mediator with you.
     I come to you now with Jesus,
     and I ask you for the grace
     to know Jesus better,
     so that I can love him more
     and follow him more closely.

5. To recall from time to time during the day: "Thank you, Father; thank you, Jesus." Or: "Jesus, help me to know you better."

Week Three, Day Six:

1. Read the Christmas story, Luke 2:1-20.

2. The grace to ask for: to know Jesus better so that I can love him more and follow him more closely.

3. Points to help to contemplate Jesus in the mystery of his birth:

(i) "She gave birth to her first-born son, and wrapped him in swaddling cloths, and laid him in a manger, because there was no place for them in the inn" (verse 7).

(ii) "And the angel said to the shepherds, 'Be not afraid; for behold, I bring you news of a great joy which will come to all the people; for to you is born this day in the city of David a Savior, who is Christ the Lord. And this will be a sign for you: you will find a babe wrapped in swaddling cloths and lying in a manger'" (verses 10-12).

(iii) "Mary kept all these things, pondering them in her heart" (verse 19).

Note: You may want to make this contemplation by simply visualizing, imagining, the Christmas scene with Joseph, Mary, and the infant Jesus, and then just entering into that scene in a loving and prayerful way.

4. Prayer:
Jesus, help me to know you better.
With the eyes of faith and love,
I see you, Jesus, in your mother's arms,
a little baby, born for me.
Thank you, Jesus.
Amen.

5. To plant in your heart to recall during the day: "Thank you, Jesus." Or: perhaps a line or a verse from a Christmas hymn, such as "O come let us adore him, Christ the Lord."

Week Three, Day Seven:

1. Read the story of Jesus' baptism in the Jordan River: Luke 3:16-22.

2. Ask Jesus for the grace to know him better in this mystery of his baptism and his anointing by the Holy Spirit, so that you can love him more and follow him more closely.

3. Points to help to contemplate Jesus' baptism and the descent of the Holy Spirit upon him:
>   (i) "Now when all the people were baptized, and when Jesus also had been baptized and was praying, heaven was opened, and the Holy Spirit descended upon him in bodily form, as a dove" (verses 21-22).
>   (ii) "And a voice came from heaven, 'You are my beloved Son, with you I am well pleased'" (verse 22).
>   (iii) "John answered them, 'I baptize you with water; but he who is mightier that I is coming, the thong of whose sandals I am not worthy to untie. He will baptize you with the Holy Spirit and with fire'" (verse 16).

4. Prayer:
>   Lord Jesus, after your baptism by John,
>   the Holy Spirit descended on you,
>   and the Father expressed his love for you
>   and his delight in you.
>   Anoint me with your Holy Spirit.
>   and with the gift of knowing you better.
>   I want to love you more
>   and to follow you more closely.
>   Thank you, Jesus,
>   because I am with and in you,
>   and you in me.

And the Father loves me and delights in me
because I am with you
Thank you, Father.
Amen.

5. To recall during the day: "Send you Spirit." Or: "Thank you, Father; thank you, Jesus; thank you, Holy Spirit."

WEEK FOUR:

Praying for a New Outpouring of the Holy Spirit and the Gifts of Prayer

The main purpose of the FOURTH WEEK is to pray for a new outpouring of the Holy Spirit. I can receive a new outpouring of the Holy Spirit as often as the Lord wills. Even if I have already received "the baptism in the Holy Spirit," I can receive a new and great outpouring of the Spirit again, or several more times in my life. Traditionally, we call the first such outpouring "the baptism in the Holy Spirit." I can, also, receive a second, a third, and so on.

This lesson comes on the same day that the daily prayer outline has proposed praying about, contemplating, the descent of the Holy Spirit on Jesus at his baptism in the Jordan. After his water-baptism by John, Jesus is anointed by the Holy Spirit; he receives a new outpouring of the Holy Spirit.

My prayer today participates in, shares in, the mystery of Jesus' own anointing by the Spirit. I ask Jesus to anoint me with his Holy Spirit and with the gifts I need, and especially with gifts of prayer.

READING: PRAYING FOR THE HOLY SPIRIT AND HIS GIFTS

a. A New Outpouring of the Holy Spirit

Jesus himself, already, as God, on with God-the-Holy-Spirit, received a new outpouring of the Holy Spirit (Luke 3:21-22 and 4:1 and 14). Our blessed Lady, already "full of grace" (Luke 1:28), was with the apostles in the upper room on the day of Pentecost, and received a new in-filling of the Holy Spirit (Acts 1:14 and 2:4). And even within a few days of Pentecost, the Holy Spirit came anew on the apostles and disciples (Acts 4:23-31).

Both the Father and Jesus send the Holy Spirit: "The Counsellor, the Holy Spirit, whom the Father will send in my name" (John 14:25), and "He [Jesus] will baptize you with the Holy Spirit and with fire" (Matthew 3:11). This is what we ask.

The Holy Spirit is not poured out on us because we are worthy: "The promise [i.e. the Holy Spirit] is to you and to your children and to all who are far off, everyone whom the Lord our God calls to him" (Acts 2:39). "Behold I send the promise of my Father upon you" (Luke 24:49). "I will pour out my Spirit upon all—even upon my slaves, men and women" (Acts 2:17-18).

Nor is the Holy Spirit given in proportion to our worthiness, but abundantly: "It is not by measure that he [God] gives the Spirit" (John 3:34).

In praying for a new outpouring of the Holy Spirit we can ask for specific gifts, especially for the gifts of our state in life. For example, a person who is a teacher can ask for the charism of teaching. A doctor or a nurse could ask for the charism of healing. A charism is a special grace not given to everyone, a grace for the up-building of the body of Christ which we are. And we can hopefully expect the Lord to give us the gifts that we most need or that best fit our lives and our places in the body of Christ, the Church. So we will "walk not after the flesh, but after the Spirit" (Romans 8:1).

One gift for which we can all ask is the gift of prayer, that is, the gift of a personal loving relationship with Jesus—a knowing of Jesus, in love. In the Holy Trinity, the Father looks at Jesus his Son; Jesus looks at his Father. This mutual knowledge-in-love is personified in the Holy Spirit. He is Knowledge-in-Love. He it is who "dwells with you and will be in you" (John 14:17).

Frequently, those baptized in the Holy Spirit first realize that something has happened when they find the words of holy scripture leaping at them off the page. Another possible confirmation is the gift of tongues.

b. The Gift of Tongues

Many people have found the gift of tongues to be the single biggest help toward contemplative prayer, because the gift of tongues is a type of contemplation. When I contemplate silently, I look—with the eyes of faith—at the Lord, without meditating, without concepts. Contemplation in silence is a non-conceptual prayer, a conceptless looking with love at the Lord. Praying in tongues is, also, a non-conceptual prayer, a conceptless looking with love at the Lord.

When I speak or sing in tongues, I do not speak or sing a language, at least not in the vast majority of cases. Scientific analysis of tapes of tongue-speaking has never found the structure of a real language. When I pray in tongues, I babble; linguistically, I am saying or singing gibberish. The meaning is not in the sounds, as though they were words that represented concepts. The meaning of prayer in tongues lies in the heart, because prayer in tongues is non-conceptual. The sounds are not words; they have no conceptual meaning. They are just meaningless syllables.

Praying in tongues is vocalized non-conceptual prayer. It is "noisy contemplation."

There is an analogy between praying in tongues and saying the rosary in such a way as to contemplate the mysteries of the life of Jesus while saying the words. When I say the rosary, I "meditate" on the various mysteries; in reality, I look at—contemplate—Jesus or his mother in the different mysteries. I say the words, but I pay no attention to their meaning; my attention is not on the words I say but on the Lord at whom I am looking. The words might as well be just sounds. Praying in tongues is similar; I pay no attention to the nonsense syllables I say or sing because I am looking at the Lord, contemplating him.

Many people who have the gift of tongues begin daily personal prayer with a brief period—perhaps thirty seconds or a few minutes—of praying in tongues. In that way, they enter consciously in to the Lord's presence; they enter easily into contemplative prayer and then remain there silently. Some use the gift of tongues more in their personal prayer, even much more.

The principal use of the gift of tongues is not, as many suppose, in prayer groups or in charismatic conferences. It is in personal prayer (1 Corinthians 14:2-4).

The principal use of the gift o tongues is not, as many suppose, in prayer groups or in charismatic conferences. It is in personal prayer (1 Corinthians 14:2-4).

If I do not have the gift of tongues yet, and would like to have it, how can I receive it?

By asking. When you pray for a new outpouring of the Holy Spirit, ask the Lord, either out loud or silently in your heart, for the gift of tongues. Then do this:

(i) Look at the Lord with the eyes of faith,

(ii) and begin to sing or to say syllables to him, syllables that make no sense, like a baby that has not learned to talk yet;

(iii) then let it flow. If you find yourself praying in sounds you don't understand, that is the gift of tongues.

c. Praying for a New Outpouring of the Holy Spirit

How should you pray for a new outpouring of the Holy Spirit? And when, and where?

(i) Where? Choose somewhere private or relatively private—your room, or an empty or fairly empty church, for example. Take a Bible, or at least a New Testament, with you.

(ii) When? Sometime after you have read the reading up to this point—perhaps this evening, or during your personal prayer time today or tomorrow.

(iii) What should you do? Choose a reverent body posture; you are going to ask for a big grace, and for gifts of the Spirit, especially for gifts of knowing the Lord through love in prayer. Kneel, or sit reverently; at any rate, put yourself in a posture respectful of the Lord. You might hold out your hands in front of your body, palms up, in a gesture or receptiveness. Then, in any way or ways that seem appropriate to you, ask the Lord to fill you with his Holy Spirit.

You might sing a hymn, if you know one, asking the Holy Spirit to come to you. For example, "Come, Holy Ghost," or "Spirit of the Living God, Fall Afresh on Me." Or perhaps you know a hymn to the Lord asking him to pour out his Spirit on you, such as, "Send Your Spirit." Pray in your own words; ask the Lord to fill you with his Spirit and with his gifts. Do not be afraid of repeating the same words over and over. Pray simply, in a childlike way. If you have the gift of praying in tongues, pray for the Spirit using the gift of tongues.

And ask him for the gifts of his Spirit. For gifts of prayer: of knowing him through love, of contemplation, of prayerfully believing in him and hoping in him and loving him, of prayerfully and effectively interceding with him for other persons, for the gift of tongues. If you already have the gift of tongues, use it to pray for a new outpouring of the Spirit with his gifts. If you have never prayed in tongues, but would like to, then ask for that gift. Look at the Lord with love, open your mouth, and speak or sing (on one note, to begin with) some syllables that make no sense, to get unblocked and to start. Then let it flow. Be sure to sing to the Lord. It pleases him. You may feel foolish, but that is just your pride; you will get over that. Pray in tongues to the Lord, with love, and freely. If you find yourself speaking or singing to the Lord in a language you do not understand, that *is* the gift of tongues.

Pray for the other gifts that you need or can use in serving the Lord, and pray for an increase in any gifts you already have. If you teach, pray for the gift of teaching. If you are a doctor or a nurse or a counsellor or in any healing ministry, pray for the gift of praying for healing for those whom you serve. Pray for the gift of having the Bible speak to you strongly, and of finding the right Bible passage at the right time. You might want to pray for gifts of administration, or of service, or of public speaking, or of studying. Whatever you need, and whatever the Lord leads you to ask for.

Remain a while in silence. Let the Lord fill you with his Spirit. Let him do what he wants, give you what he wants to give you, speak to your heart in words or thoughts or in more mysterious and silent, secret ways, or through a passage that he may lead you to in the Bible.

Finish by thanking the Lord. Thank him for hearing your prayer and for answering it. If you feel, have felt, nothing, thank him just the same.

Thank you, Lord,
for pouring out on me your Holy Spirit—
your Spirit of faith, of hope, of love,
your Spirit of prayer.
Thank you for your gifts.

Thank you especially, Lord,
for your gift of yourself, to me, now,
through your Holy Spirit.
Amen.

d. The outlines for daily prayer during the week continue the series of contemplations, begun on the fifth day of the past week with the contemplation on the Incarnation, of the events in the life, death and resurrection of Jesus. This series of contemplations continues until almost the end of the prayer course. The coming week's daily prayer concentrates on the public life of Jesus. The grace to be asked for is, especially, to know Jesus better.

The events of Jesus' life, though historically in the past, are, in the order of grace, present and effective. In contemplating any of these events we can receive the grace of that particular mystery, the grace of that revelation, in a powerful way. We look at Jesus and he is revealed to us.

DAILY PRAYER FOR WEEK FOUR:

Knowing Jesus Better

(Note: If you have the gift of tongues, use it at least a little every day in your personal prayer.)

Week Four, Day One:

1. Read the scripture text, Luke 4:1-13, the temptations of Jesus.

2. Ask for the grace I want: to understand Satan's tactics, and to know Jesus better and to understand his ways so that I can love him more and follow him more closely.
3. Points to help in contemplating Jesus tempted by Satan and answering him:
   (i) The devil tempts Jesus to put high value on material things, but Jesus affirms the priority of the spiritual (verses 3—4).
   (ii) The devil tempts Jesus to seek the glory of this world, but Jesus gives all the glory to the Father (verses 5—8).
   (iii) The devil tempts Jesus to pride, but Jesus refutes him, saying that pride puts God to the test (verses 9—12).
   Notice Satan's tactics: he leads us to seek riches and honors, and from there to pride and the other vices. Jesus leads us to put spiritual things first, not to seek our glory but the glory of God, and from there to humility and all the other virtues.

4. Prayer:
   Lord Jesus, help me to know Satan's tactics
   and to resist them.

Help me to resist the attraction
of the riches and honors
and glory of this world.
I want to be with you,
free from attachment to riches,
free from attachment to honors,
lowly, reverent, humble, and free like you.
Jesus, teach me your ways.
Amen.

5. To put in your heart to recall during the day: "Teach me your ways." Or: "I love you, Jesus, and I choose you."

Week Four, Day Two:

1. Read Luke 4:14-21: Jesus begins his ministry and describes himself in terms of the book of the prophet Isaiah.

2. Ask for the grace I want: to know Jesus better, so that I can love him more, and follow him more closely.

3. Points to help contemplate Jesus:
    (i) ". . . returned in the power of the Spirit . . . and he taught in all their synagogues" (verses 14—15).
    (ii) "And he stood up to read . . . 'The Spirit of the Lord is upon me, because he has anointed me to preach good news to the poor. He has sent me to proclaim release to the captives and recovering of sight to the blind, to set at liberty those who are oppressed, to proclaim the acceptable year of the Lord'" (verses 18—19).
    (iii) "Today this scripture has been fulfilled in your hearing" (verse 21).

4. Prayer:
>   Lord Jesus, teach me to know you better,
>   as anointed in your Spirit by your Father
>   to speak the good news to me,
>   to set me free,
>   to open my eyes so that I may see.
>   Help me, Jesus, to understand
>   who you are for me.
>   Amen.

5. To recall during the day: "Help me to know you better."
Or: "He has sent me to bring the good news to the poor."

Week Four, Day Three:

1. Read the beatitudes in Luke 6:17-26.

2. Ask Jesus for the grace that I want: to know him better through his teaching, so that I can love him more, and follow him more closely.

3. Points to help to know Jesus better through his teaching:
>   (i) "Blessed are you poor, for yours is the kingdom of God" (verse 21).
>   (ii) "Blessed are you that weep now, for you shall laugh" (verse 22).

Or, instead, you might want to take the beatitudes as they are found in Matthew's Gospel, 5:3-11. You could apply each beatitude in turn to Jesus, seeing not only how it forms part of his teaching, but how it applies to him.

4. Prayer:
  Lord Jesus, teach me your ways.
  Teach me yourself.
  You yourself are the fulfillment
  of the beatitudes.
  Teach me to understand you,
  to know you better,
  to be like you, your disciple.
  Amen.

5. To recall during the day: "Teach me your ways." Or: "Teach me to know you better."

Week Four, Day Four:

1. Read Jesus' teaching about the law of love in Luke 6:27—36.

2. Ask for the grace I want:
  Lord Jesus, help me to know you better
  through your teaching about love,
  so that I can love you more
  and follow you more closely.

3. Points to help you to contemplate Jesus in his teaching on the law of love:
  (i) "Love your enemies, do good to those who hate you, bless those who curse you, pray for those who abuse you" (verses 27—28).
  (ii) "Love your enemies, and do good, and lend, expecting nothing in return" (verse 35).
  (iii) "Be merciful, even as your Father is merciful" (verse 38).
    See not only how Jesus teaches about love, but how his teaching describes himself and much about how he loves.

55

4. Prayer:
Lord Jesus, help me to know you better,
through your teaching on love,
through your love for me,
through my love for you.

5. To recall during the day: "Thank you, Jesus, for loving me."
Or: "Help me to know you better."

Week Four, Day Five:

1. Read about how Jesus heals in Luke 7:1—16.

2. Ask for the grace that you want:
Jesus, that I may know you better,
so that I can love you more
and follow you more closely.

3. Points to help to contemplate Jesus' healing. The scripture text describes two healings: the healing of the centurion's slave and the raising up from the dead of the widow's son. Choose one of these two healings as the matter for your prayer. You might pay particular attention to:
(i) the love and the compassion with which Jesus heals;
(ii) the power with which he heals, the power of his love;
(iii) how Jesus heals in response to an expressed need, spoken or not spoken.

4. Prayer:
Lord Jesus, thank you for your love,
for the healing power of your love.
Help me, Jesus, to receive your healing love,
to accept your love,
to respond to your love.
Amen.

5. To recall during the day: "Heal me by your love." Or: "Jesus, that I may know you better."

Week Four, Day Six:

1. Read what Jesus teaches about faith in him in Luke 8:22—25.

2. Ask for the grace that I want:
    Jesus, help me to know you better
    through faith in your relationship with me
    so that I can love you more
    and follow you more closely.
    Jesus, increase my trust in you.

3. Points to help to contemplate Jesus:
    (i) "Jesus got into the boat with his disciples" (verse 22).
    (ii) "As they sailed he fell asleep, and a storm of wind came down on the lake, and they were filling with water and were in danger. And they went and woke him, saying, 'Master, Master we are perishing.' And he awoke and rebuked the wind and the raging waves; and they ceased, and there was a calm" (verses 23—24).
    (iii) "And he said to them, 'Where is your faith?'" (verse 25).

4. Prayer:
    Lord Jesus, I believe in you.
    Strengthen my faith.
    I trust you, Jesus,
    to calm any storm in my life.
    I cry out to you now, Jesus, to help me.
    Increase my trust in you.
    Amen.

5. To recall during the day: "Jesus, increase my faith in you." Or: "Jesus, I trust you."

Week Four, Day Seven:

1. Read what Jesus teaches about following him in Luke 9:57—62.

2. Ask for the grace that I want:
    Jesus, give me the grace to know you so well
    that I will always love you
    and follow you without ever looking back.

3. Points to help contemplate Jesus:
    (i) "As they were going along the road, a man said to him, 'I will follow you wherever you go.' And Jesus said to him, 'Foxes have holes, and birds of the air have nests, but the Son of Man has nowhere to lay his head'" (verses 57—58).
    (ii) "To another he said, 'Follow me.' But he said, 'Lord, let me first go and bury my father.' But he said to him, 'Leave the dead to bury their own dead; but as for you, go and proclaim the kingdom of God'" (verses 59—60).
    (iii) "Another said, 'I will follow you, Lord, but let me first say farewell to those at my home.' Jesus said to him, 'No one who puts his hand to the plough and looks back is fit for the kingdom of God'" (verses 61—62).

4. Prayer:
    Lord Jesus, help me to understand
    Your teaching here about following you.
    Help me to understand in what ways
    it applies to me.

Teach me what it means to follow you.
Help me to love you more
so I can follow you more completely.
Help me to know you better
so I can love you more.
Amen.

5. To recall during the day: "Jesus, I will follow you wherever you go." Or: "I have decided to follow Jesus."

LORD JESUS, TEACH ME TO PRAY

WEEK FIVE:

Prayerfully Entering into Jesus'
Suffering and Death;
Contemplation; Centering Prayer

The FIFTH WEEK prepares for the daily prayer for the coming week, on the Last Supper and on the suffering and death of Jesus. It also contains a reading on contemplation that includes an instruction on centering prayer.

READING ON CONTEMPLATIVE PRAYER

a. Contemplation means looking at the Lord with love. Contemplation is a way of knowing; I can know the Lord through contemplation—not the way I know data or facts or some truth, but the way I know a person. Through contemplating Jesus, I come to know him better—not to know more about him through study, but to know him better through love.

To know a person differs from knowing about that person. I do want to know as much as I can about one who loves me and whom I love. But beyond that I want to know the person better. Jesus knows me perfectly, accepts me totally, loves me intensely and calls me by name. And he leads me to love him, and to know him better through love—through his love of me and through my loving response to his love.

Knowledge through love, then, is not abstract. The knowledge through love that comes from and that constitutes contemplation is often obscure, dark, vague, shadowy—but not abstract. Contemplation is lovingly knowing a person, this particular person, Jesus present for me here and now.

Contemplation is an experience of Jesus, of his presence and love and care—not only, nor primarily, intellectual experience, but affective experience, of the heart. Contemplation is affective knowledge, a knowing that takes place through being loved by Jesus and through loving him back.

Feelings, then, count. Sometimes, of course, I can and must pray in dryness in a kind of desert, without any special feelings, and perhaps feeling out of touch with the Lord. However, ordinarily, my contemplating Jesus will involve me to some extent at a feeling level, and I will have the spiritual taste that comes with love.

The grace for which I ask during this week is to know Jesus better as I watch him at the Last Supper and during his passion and death. Why did Jesus arrange this supper during which he gave himself to us under the form of bread and wine? Why did he allow himself to be taken, tortured, crucified? The answer is clearly given in Hebrews: "He brings a new covenant, as the mediator, only so that the people who were called to an eternal inheritance may actually receive what was promised: his death took place to cancel the sins that infringed the earlier covenant" (Hebrews 9:15). So at the supper Jesus remakes the covenant we have with God, which had been broken on our side: "'If you obey my voice and hold fast to my covenant, you of all nations shall be my very own, a consecrated nation.' Then all the people answered as one: 'All that Yahweh has said, we will do'" (Exodus 19:5—8). Jesus remakes that broken covenant: "This cup is the new covenant of my blood which will be poured out for you" (Luke 22:20). Hebrews 8:6—12 is a powerful description of this "better covenant of which he is the mediator" (verse 6b).

Jesus goes willingly to his passion and death: "I lay down my life—no one takes it from me" (John 10:17—18). He does so in order to restore the obedience of the covenant. "All that Yahweh says, he will do." "I lay it [my life] down of my own free will—and this is the command I have been given by my Father" (John 10:18). "I am doing exactly what the Father told me" (John 14:31).

Jesus lovingly suffers to restore us to union with his Father. But he suffers in darkness, in faith, in anguish of soul. It was difficult for him to die for me. "There is a baptism I must receive, and how great is my distress until it is over!" (Luke 22:42). He lost sight of his Father: "My God, my God, why have you deserted me?" (Matthew 27:46). At his baptism he had heard his Father say, "This is my Son, the Beloved . . . " (Matthew 3:17). Now, in his dereliction he hears only the mocking echo: "Let him save himself if he is the Christ of God, the Chosen One" (Luke 23:35).

I contemplate Jesus, knowing that he said: "A man can have no greater love than to lay down his life for his friends. You are my friends" (John 15:13—14).

b. Centering Prayer

Contemplation can take the form of centering prayer, in which I center my awareness on Jesus in my heart. Centering prayer centers not on a word or phrase, such as the name of Jesus, but centers through a word or phrase on the person—repeating the name "Jesus" over and over slowly, not with my lips but silently in my heart, centering on the person my heart calls and rests in.

Or I can use the "Jesus prayer," the "prayer of the pilgrim": "Lord Jesus Christ, have mercy on me, a sinner," repeating the phrase over and over slowly in my heart. But the focus here is on the Lord Jesus Christ, not a technique. This way of praying, to repeat in one's heart an ejaculation or the name of Jesus, is, surely, a good way to pray; it can lead to real contemplation. But contemplation itself, that mysterious and conceptless interpersonal encounter with Jesus Christ, remains his gift, his to give, and mine to receive—not to conquer or to achieve through technique, nor somehow to win or merit.

DAILY PRAYER FOR WEEK FIVE:

The Last Supper and the Passion and Death of Jesus

Week Five, Day One:

1. Read the account of the Last Supper, where Jesus, anticipating the sacrifice of the cross, takes bread, saying, "This is my body," and wine, saying, "This cup is the new covenant in my blood": Luke 22:14—23.

2. Ask for the grace that I want:
   Lord Jesus,
   help me to know you better
   in the mystery of the Last Supper,
   in the mystery of the Holy Eucharist,
   in the mystery of your giving yourself up
   for me, to me.
   And help me to love you more
   so that I can follow you more closely.
   Especially, Jesus, help me to enter into
   the mystery of your suffering and death.

3. Points to help to contemplate Jesus:
   (i) "When the hour came, Jesus sat at table, and the apostles with him. And he said to them, 'I have earnestly desired to eat this Passover with you before I suffer'" (verses 14—15).
   (ii) "He took bread, and when he had given thanks he broke it and gave it to them, saying, 'This is my body which is given for you. Do this in remembrance of me'" (verse 19).
   (Note: In the RSV translation, the last half of verse 19 and all of verse 20 are at the bottom of the page.)

4. Prayer:
    Lord Jesus, help me to know you better,
    to enter into your heart and feelings
    as you prepare to suffer and die.
    Take me into your heart,
    into your suffering.
    Unite my heart to yours.
    Amen.

5. To recall during the day: "This is my body which will be given for you." Or: "Take me into your heart."

Week Five, Day Two:

1. Read Jesus' teaching at the Last Supper about humility and service in Luke 22:24—28. Jesus not only teaches us how to act; he teaches us about himself, what he is like.

2. Ask for the grace I want:
    Jesus, help me to know you better
    through your teaching here
    so that I can love you more
    and be united with you
    as you face your suffering and death,
    and so that I can follow you more closely.

3. Points to help contemplate Jesus:
    (i) "The kings of the Gentiles exercise lordship over them; and those in authority over them are called benefactors. But not so with you; rather the greatest among you must become as the youngest, and the leader as one who serves" (verses 25—26).
    (ii) "For which is the greater, one who sits at table, or one who serves? Is it not the one who sits at table? But I am

among you as one who serves" (verse 27).
(iii) "You are those who have continued with me in my trials" (verse 28).

4. Prayer:
Jesus, I want to continue with you
in your trials, as you prepare
to suffer and to die,
to suffer for me,
to die so that I can have eternal life.
You make yourself
the lowest and the smallest,
a servant,
even to suffering and death,
for love of me.
Amen.

5. To put in your heart to recall during the day: "Jesus, teach me to know you better in your love for me." Or: "You are those who have continued with me in my trials."

Week Five, Day Three:

1. Read Luke 22:39—46, Jesus' agony in Gethsemane.

2. Ask Jesus for the grace that you want:
Jesus, I want to enter into your sufferings,
into your agony, into your heart,
to be with you in your agony.
Give me the grace to know you better
in your agony in the garden,
to love you more,
to follow you more closely.

3. Points to contemplate Jesus in agony:
(i) "Jesus prayed, 'Father, if you are willing, remove this cup from me; nevertheless, not my will, but yours be done'" (verse 42).
(ii) "And being in agony he prayed more earnestly; and his sweat became like great drops of blood falling down upon the ground" (verse 44).
(iii) "And when he rose from prayer, he came to the disciples and found them sleeping. He said, 'Why do you sleep? Rise and pray that you may not enter into temptation'" (verse 45—46).

4. Prayer:
Lord Jesus,
I want to be with you in your agony.
Keep me with you there today.
Amen.

5. To recall during the day: "Jesus, I want to be with you."
Or: "Not my will, but yours be done."

Week Five, Day Four:

1. Read Luke 23:13—15, Jesus is unjustly condemned to death.

2. I ask for the grace I want:
Jesus help me to know you better in your
passion, to be united with you in your suffering.

3. Points to help contemplate Jesus:
(i) "Pilate said, 'Nothing deserving death has been done by him. I will therefore chastise him and release him'" (verses 16—17).
(ii) "But they all cried out together, 'Away with this man,

and release to us Barabbas.' Pilate addressed them once more, desiring to release Jesus, but they shouted out, 'Crucify him, crucify him'" (verses 18 and 19—20).
(iii) "A third time he said to them, 'Why, what evil has he done? I have found in him no crime deserving death; I will therefore chastise him and release him.' But they were urgent, demanding with loud cries that he should be crucified. And their voices prevailed. So Pilate gave sentence that their demand should be granted" (verses 21—24).

4. Prayer:
Jesus,
I see you after having been beaten,
crowned with thorns,
standing before the crowd.
I want to be with you in your suffering
and in your rejection by your own people.
Put my heart next to yours.
Let me be with you in your suffering.
Amen.

5. During the day you might try to recall to mind from time to time and image or picture of Jesus crowned with thorns. Or turn to the Lord from time to time and say, "Jesus, I love you."

Week Five, Day Five:

1. Read Luke 23:26—38, Jesus on the way to Calvary.

2. Pray for the grace I want:
Jesus, I want to be with you
as you carry your cross,
to know you better,
to share your feelings and your sufferings,

to love you more
and to follow you more closely.

3. Points to help contemplate Jesus on his way to be crucified:
(i) "They led him away" (verse 26).
(ii) "They seized one Simon of Cyrene, who was coming
in from the country, and laid on him the cross, to carry it
behind Jesus" (verse 26).
(iii) "And there followed behind him a great multitude of
the people, and of women who bewailed and lamented
him" (verse 27).

4. Prayer:
Jesus, I see you carrying your cross
on the way to Calvary.
I want to be with you,
to be Simon of Cyrene helping you,
to somehow be with you in your suffering,
in your carrying the cross.
Thank you for loving me,
for suffering for me,
for carrying your cross out of love for me.
Amen.

5. To recall during the day: perhaps an image or a picture of
Jesus carrying his cross; or an image or a picture of Jesus'
face or head crowned with thorns. Or: "Jesus, I love you."

Week Five, Day Six:

1. Read Luke 23:39—43, Jesus is crucified.

2. I ask for the grace I want:
   Lord Jesus, I want to know you better
   in your suffering and death on the cross
   so that I can love you more
   and follow you more closely.

3. Points for contemplating Jesus crucified:
   (i) "And when they came to the place which is called the Skull, there they crucified him" (verse 33).
   (ii) "Jesus said, 'Father, forgive them; for they know not what they do'" (verse 34).
   (iii) "The rulers scoffed at him, saying, 'He saved others; let him save himself, if he is the Christ of God, his Chosen One!' The soldiers also mocked him, coming up and offering him vinegar, and saying, 'If you are the King of the Jews, save yourself!'" (verses 35—37).

4. Prayer:
   Jesus, I see you crucified.
   You forgive those who kill you
   and who make fun of you,
   and you do not come down from the cross.
   Lord Jesus, I love you and I adore you.
   Amen.

5. To recall during the day: a picture or an image of Jesus crucified. Or: "Jesus, I love you and I adore you."

Week Five, Day Seven:

1. Read Luke 23:44—49, the death of Jesus.

2. I ask for the grace I want:
   Jesus, give me the grace to know you better
   in your dying on the cross for me,
   and help me to love you more
   and to follow you more closely.

3. Points to help contemplate Jesus dying on the cross:
   (i) "There was darkness over the whole land, while the sun's light failed; and the curtain of the temple was torn in two. Then Jesus, crying with a loud voice, said, 'Father, into your hands I commend my spirit.' And having said this, he breathed his last" (verses 44—46).
   (ii) "When the centurion saw what had taken place, he praised God, and said, 'Certainly this man was innocent!'" (verse 47).
   (iii) "All his acquaintances and the women who had followed him from Galilee stood at a distance and saw these things" (verse 49).

4. Make up your own prayer; or perhaps just remain silent before the cross.

5. To recall during the day: an image or a picture of Jesus crucified. Or: "Jesus, I love you and I adore you.

WEEK SIX:

Entering into the Joy of Jesus' Resurrection;
The Discernment of Spirits and
Making Decisions

The SIXTH WEEK includes a reading on the discernment of spirits and on using discernment in making decisions. And it prepares the way for the week's daily prayer on the resurrection of Jesus and his appearances to his disciples.

But first of all, how did your prayer go last week? How did you feel in your prayer? Not all negative feelings in prayer are necessarily undesirable. They can be quite helpful and they can be truly from the Lord. In praying about the passion, for example, I can feel sadness that Jesus is suffering; I can feel an anguish that shares in his own anguish during his passion. I can even have tears for what he goes through for my sins. I can feel a fear of, or a repugnance to, meditating on the passion. These emotions can unite me more closely to Jesus in my prayer. They are good, not bad.

The criterion for evaluating thoughts and especially feelings in prayer is this: Did they or did they not give me a greater facility in relating to Jesus? Did they unite me more closely, more easily with him? Some people may think their prayer has gone poorly when in fact it went well.

READING ON SPIRITUAL DISCERNMENT

"Give your servant a heart to understand how to discern between good and evil" (1 Kings 3:9). This was Solomon's prayer. The Lord was pleased to give him "a discerning judgment" (*ibid.*, verse 11). Discernment—whether judging good from evil, or a better good from a lesser one, or finding what God wants us to do in any situation—can take place only in prayer. Saint Paul is clear on this: "An unspiritual person is one who does not accept anything of the Spirit of God: he sees it as nonsense; it is beyond his understanding because it can only be understood by means of the Spirit. A spiritual man, on the other hand, is able to judge the value of everything... We are those who have the mind of Christ" (1 Corinthians 2:14—16). To have the mind of Christ: only in prayer can we know Jesus, know what is his mind on any subject.

a. Spiritual discernment is that prayerful process by which I examine, through love and in the light of faith, the nature of my experience: Does this particular impulse or idea or plan or project or word come from the Lord or not? Is it from the Spirit of Jesus or from some other source? Knowing where a particular thought or plan or word comes from will help me in making decisions; I want to follow up and carry out what comes from the Holy Spirit. And I want to reject and avoid what comes from the other spirits.

Paul practices the discernment of spirits with the various communities to whom he writes. And he preaches discernment (Philippians 1:9—11). Be "led by the Spirit of God" (Romans 8:14); "Walk as children of the light and try to have an interior grasp of what is the Lord's will" (Ephesians 5:8—10; see 5:17). Paul's chief criterion for discernment is a person's relation to Jesus Christ (1 Corinthians 12:3, 23:3). The same is true of John's gospel and the letters of John: "By this you know the Spirit of God: every spirit that confesses that Jesus Christ has come in the flesh is of God, and every spirit that does not confess Jesus Christ is not of God" (1 John 4:2—3).

Very often, by best criterion for judging the origin of a thought or a proposed action or an inner urging will be what Saint Ignatius Loyola calls "consolation." What does he mean by consolation? I have consolation whenever I begin to be aflame with love for the Lord, when I cannot love anything or anyone on earth except in the Lord and Creator of them all, or when I pour out tears of sorrow for the sufferings and death of the Lord or for my sins or the sins of the world. Or, finally, consolation can be any felt increase of faith, of hope and trust in the Lord, of love, and also every inner gladness that attracts me to the things of the Spirit and that brings me interior repose and peace in the Lord. Briefly, a thought or plan or feeling or impulse brings me consolation when it brings me closer to the Lord, gives me a certain facility in relating to him, in finding him, in being united with him.

For those trying to live a Christian life, trying to live according to the Holy Spirit, consolation is a useful criterion for evaluating interior experience. When I am face to face with the Lord in prayer, looking at him with the eyes of faith and trust and love, how comfortable with him do I feel in terms of this particular idea, project, urging? When I contemplate Jesus, offering him this particular thought of impulse, how do I feel in terms of my relationship with him? Do I feel a certain rightness, a certain peace, or perhaps even gladness or joy, when I propose this particular thing to the Lord in contemplation? It gives me what Ignatius calls consolation, then that consolation is a sign that it comes form him.

Ignatius calls "desolation" whatever seems to separate me from the Lord: temptations to sin or to move away from the Lord in any way, gloominess of heart and mind, confusion, whatever causes distrust in the Lord, lack of faith and hope, coldness of love. Briefly, desolation is whatever is contrary to consolation. Is desolation what John of the Cross calls "the dark night"? No. I can, in the dark night of prayer, have either desolation or consolation at different times. The dark night often is, in fact, a time or real peace and rest in the Lord, of being content to be united with him in the dark, and so it is a time of consolation.

My discernment will not be infallible. It, too, often needs to be discerned, to be monitored, evaluated, and perhaps revised. In discernment, and especially in discerning a discernment itself, sometimes a prayerful friend, a regular confessor, or a spiritual director can be helpful.

b. Discernment and Decision-Making

Let us say that I want to discern God's will for me in an important matter. I have already gathered the pertinent facts, the relevant information. Perhaps, as needed, I have consulted one or two other persons. At any rate, I now have an adequate grasp of the problem. But I remain unable to come to a decision; I still do not know what the Lord wants me to do in this particular matter. I have already prayed for the Lord's light and guidance in marshalling the data, in consulting persons or books or documents, in going over pros and cons. Now, I take my decision-to-be-made explicitly to the Lord and see what he wants me to do.

Jesus is the Lord of my life, and I want to bring my decision to him, to make my decision under his lordship. In a brief period of contemplation, of looking with faith and love at the Lord, I try to think through the matter with him—not in a logical and highly reasoned way, but mulling things over with the Lord, in the prayer zone of his love for me. With Jesus, looking him in the eye as it were, contemplating him, I ponder my possible alternative decisions, my options in the case under consideration. I lift up to Jesus, in turn, the various possible ways I could decide. I see how I feel about each one in terms of my relationship with God.

Ordinarily, over a period of time relative to the importance of the decision in question, I will come to a conclusion. I lift up to the Lord all the options, discerning as to the source (good spirit or not) of each one, for a few minutes once or twice every day. I do this in an explicit way, taking Jesus' loving care for me seriously, trying truly to find out what he wants, consulting him with seriousness and with trust.

After a certain amount of this, or perhaps right at the beginning and from then on, I will feel consolation with regard to one of the options. When I "look the Lord in the eye" about one possible decision, I will consistently feel a kind of fittingness, a rightness, that this is right. Or a consistent peace and interior harmony. Or possibly a real joy and gladness of heart. This is a sign that the particular option is from the good spirit.

The key, then, is this: How right, how comfortable in the Lord's presence, do I feel in terms of each of the options? But how can I be sure? I will probably not attain complete certainty. I can stay with my conclusion (that this particular possible decision is the one I should make) for some days, testing it, holding it up for confirmation to the Lord to see if it is really from him. If it is, the consolation will continue. I can continue for a while to discern my discernment. And then I make and carry out my decision.

If my decision involves another person, I may need to pray with that person; a husband and wife may need to come to a joint decision. In that case, they will need to discern individually, to pool the results of their prayerful discernment, and to pray together. Some decisions are group decisions and call for a discernment on the part of each member of the group.

The process of communal discernment, where two or more persons have to make the decision together, might go like this. Each one prays alone, discerning. They come together—not to discuss, but to pool, to listen to the prayerful conclusion reached by each one. Then they pray together. If unanimity is not reached, then the process can be repeated until it is, or until a vote of some kind is taken.

c. Preparation for Daily Prayer during the Week

The matter for daily prayer this week is the resurrection, the appearances of the risen Jesus to his disciples, and the sending of the Spirit at Pentecost. We can expect our prayer, then, to have a different tone or quality from last week. It should have joy and consolation.

What is the grace that I want, the grace that I ask for, for my prayer this week? It is the grace to rejoice in Jesus' resurrection, to share his resurrection gladness.

When Jesus appears to his friends after his resurrection, what does he do? He consoles them. The risen Jesus is Jesus the Consoler. He says, "Fear not." He cheers them up, not with a false optimism but by giving them real hope. He makes them happy. They are glad and joyful at his resurrection.

I want Jesus to console me in my prayer this week. To make me glad, happy, joyful in him, so that I can share in the joy of his resurrection, of his risen state.

Daily Prayer for Week Six:

Jesus Is Risen

Week Six, Day One:

1. Read Luke 24:1—12, Jesus is risen.

2. Ask Jesus for the grace you want: to rejoice in him risen, to share his gladness and joy, to receive his consoling and gladdening love, and so to grow in love for Jesus and in discipleship.

3. Points to help to contemplate Jesus risen:
   (i) "Two men stood by them in dazzling apparel and said, 'Why do you seek the living among the dead? Remember how he told you, while he was still in Galilee, that the Son of Man must be delivered into the hands of sinful men, and be crucified, and on the third day rise'" (verses 4—7).
   (ii) "Returning from the tomb, they told all this to the eleven and to all the rest" (verse 9).
   (iii) "But these words seemed to them an idle tale, and they did not believe them" (verse 11).

4. Prayer:
   Lord Jesus, you are risen
   and here with me now
   to let me share in your joy,
   to make me glad,
   to console me.
   Give me your consolation.
   I praise you, Lord, in your risen glory.
   All honor and power and glory to you.
   Amen.

5. To recall during the day: perhaps and image or a picture of the risen Jesus. Or: "All honor and power and glory to you, Jesus." Or: "Rejoice in the Lord always." Or some other hymn refrain.

Week Six, Day Two:

1. Read Luke 24:13—29, Jesus meets the two disciples on the road to Emmaus.

2. I ask for the grace that I want:
   Lord Jesus,
   give me the grace to know you better
   and to rejoice and be glad
   in you risen and present to me now.
   Help me to love you more
   and to follow you more closely.

3. Points to help to contemplate Jesus risen:
   (i) "While they were talking and discussing together, Jesus himself drew near and went with them" (verse 15).
   (ii) "And Jesus said to them, 'O foolish men, and slow of heart to believe all that the prophets have spoken! Was it not necessary that the Christ should suffer these things and enter into his glory?' And beginning with Moses and all the prophets he interpreted to them in all the scriptures the things concerning himself" (verses 25—27).
   (iii) "They constrained him, saying, 'Stay with us, for it is toward evening, and the day is now far spent.' So he went in to stay with them" (verse 29).

4. Prayer:
  Lord Jesus, you have drawn near to me
  and you are with me now in my prayer.
  Reveal to me, Jesus, the meaning of scripture,
  the meaning of this text for me now,
  for you and me together.
  Jesus, walk with me always.
  Let me always walk with you.
  Stay with me, Lord.
  Amen.

5. To recall during the day: "Stay with me, Jesus." Or a refrain or line from a resurrection or praise hymn that you can sing to Jesus. Or: "Stay with us, Lord, for it is toward evening, and the day is now far spent.

Week Six, Day Three:

1. Read the rest of the account of Jesus' meeting with the disciples on the road to Emmaus: Luke 24:30—35.

2. I ask for the grace that I want:
  Lord Jesus, give me the grace to know you,
  Risen and here with me now,
  and to share in your resurrection
  joy and gladness.
  Help me to know you better
  so that I can love you more
  and follow you more closely.

3. Points to help to contemplate Jesus:
  (i) "When he was at table with them, he took the bread and blessed and broke it, and gave it to them. And their eyes were opened, and they recognized him" (verses 30—31).

81

(ii) "They said to each other, 'Did not our hearts burn within us while he talked to us on the road, while he opened to us the scriptures?'" (verse 32).
(iii) "They told what had happened on the road, and how he was known to them in the breaking of the bread" (verse 35).

4. Prayer:
Lord Jesus, you are risen
and here with me now.
You are "at table" with me now in my prayer.
Reveal to me yourself.
Let me recognize you.
Let me know you better through love
so that I can better witness in my life
that I know you
and so lead others to know you better.
Amen.

5. To recall during the day: "Jesus, help me to recognize you."
Or a line or refrain from a resurrection or praise hymn to Jesus.

Week Six, Day Four:

1. Read Luke 24:36—43, Jesus appears to his disciples.

2. I ask for the grace that I want:
Jesus, help me to know
you better through love
and to share the joy of your resurrection
so that I can love you more
and follow you more closely.

3. Points to help to contemplate Jesus:
(i) "Jesus himself stood among them" (verse 36).
(ii) "He said to them, 'Why are you troubled, and why do questionings rise in your hearts?'" (verse 38).
(iii) "While they still disbelieved for joy, and wondered, he said to them, 'Have you anything here to eat?' They gave him a piece of broiled fish, and he took it and ate it before them" (verses 41—43).

4. Prayer:
Lord Jesus,
you yourself, risen, are here with me now.
Any troubledness I might
feel, any questionings,
I hand over to you.
And I praise you, Jesus,
for the glory and the power of
your risen presence.
Give me your gladness and joy,
the joy of your resurrection.
Amen.

5. To put in your heart to recall during the day: "Jesus, you are here." Or: "I praise you, Jesus, for the glory and the power of your resurrection.

Week Six, Day Five:

1. Read Luke 24:44—48, Jesus explains to his disciples the meaning of the scriptures.

2. I ask Jesus for the grace that I want:
Jesus, help me through this scripture
to understand you better,

to know you better through love,
so that I can love you more
and follow you more closely.

3. Points to help to contemplate Jesus risen:
   (i) "He opened their minds to understand the scriptures"
   (verse 45).
   (ii) "Thurs it is written that the Christ should suffer and
   on the third day rise from the dead" (verse 46).
   (iii) " . . . and that repentance and forgiveness of sins
   should be preached in his name to all nations, beginning
   from Jerusalem" (verse 47).

4. Prayer:
   Lord Jesus,
   show me what this scripture
   text means for me,
   for the relationship between us,
   for my union with you.
   I rejoice, Lord, in your resurrection,
   in your risen life,
   in you, here, now.
   Let my rejoicing in you, Lord,
   be a praise of you risen.
   Amen.

5. To recall during the day: "Jesus, open my heart to know
you better." Or: "Praise you, Jesus, you are risen and with
us."

Week Six, Day Six:

1. Read Luke 24:48—53.

2. I ask for the grace that I want:
   Jesus, give me the grace
   to know you better through love
   and through the gladness and joy
   of your resurrection.
   And help me to love you more
   and to follow you more closely.

3. Points to help to contemplate Jesus risen:
   (i) "You are witnesses of these things. And behold I send
   the promise of my Father upon you; but stay in the city
   until you are clothed with power from on high" (verses
   48—49).
   (ii) "Lifting up his hands, he blessed them" (verse 50).
   (iii) "They returned to Jerusalem with great joy, and were
   continually in the temple blessing God" (verses 52—53).

4. Prayer:
   Lord Jesus, thank you for being here, risen,
   with me, now.
   Thank you for your Holy Spirit in my heart.
   He makes me a witness to you,
   your witness.
   Bless me now, Jesus,
   and give me the gift of joy in you
   and the gift of praise,
   so I can joyfully praise you and the Father
   in the unity of the Holy Spirit.
   Amen.

5. To recall during the day: "Bless me, Jesus." Or: "Praise to you, Jesus."

Week Six, Day Seven:

For your prayer today, go back to one of the days this week where you experienced the Lord, and repeat the prayer of that day.

WEEK SEVEN:

Looking ahead

The SEVENTH WEEK concludes the prayer course by looking ahead and by encouraging you to make concrete plans for the future regarding your prayer life.

READING: FAITHFULNESS AND DARKNESS

a. Faithfulness to a fixed amount of time daily for personal prayer, for quiet time with the Lord, is faithfulness to him, and an expression of commitment and love.

b. If you have not experienced much dryness or aridity or darkness in prayer, you surely will. Everyone does to some extent sometimes. For many, it can last a very long time and be a habitual state of prayer. What do I do in the darkness? I try to remain in as much peace as I can, and I let the Lord love me in the darkness. I pray in the darkness and the dryness of faith, knowing that the darkness and the dryness purify my faith, my love, myself for the Lord.

c. What should you use for your daily prayer form now on?

You can use the suggested scripture texts from John's gospel to get you started. If you feel led by the Lord to stay with the resurrection theme, go straight to John, chapters 20 to 21, and then after a week or so perhaps take John, chapters 14 and 19.

After that you can start on your own. It is a good idea to prepare your point from scripture the night before, and to sleep on it—especially if you pray in the morning.

What scripture should you use when your are on your own? You could start at the beginning of a gospel and work your way through it, taking a little at a time, praying about a few verses each day. Or you could use the gospel read in Mass each day; you can always go into the sacristy and ask for the Ordo for the Masses. It gives the scripture readings for each day; you could copy them out once a week or once a month, or get them from a daily missal.

d. This course has had as its purpose to help you to pray more personally, more deeply, more freely. Now you are on your own. Be open to the way the Lord leads you in your prayer. Let the Bible speak to your heart. Let the Lord transform you through your contact with him in prayer. Launch out into the deep of the Lord's love in freedom and in trust.

DAILY PRAYER POINTS FOR FIVE MORE WEEKS:

John's gospel, chapters 14 to 21

Note: These points can be used for follow-up to the prayer course. There are enough points for five weeks. After that, or even before if you wish, you can begin to make up your own points from the gospels, working through a gospel a little at a time, or using the gospel from the Mass for the day.

Day One:

1. Read John 14:1—7.

2. The prayer for the grace that I want is always the same except for prayer about the passion and death of Jesus and prayer about his resurrection and resurrection appearances:
   Jesus, help me to know you better
   so that I can love you more
   and follow you more closely.

3. Points:
   (i) "Let not your hearts be troubled. Believe in God; believe also in me" (verse 1).
   (ii) "I am the way, the truth, and the life" (verse 6).
   (iii) "If you had known me, you would have known my Father also; henceforth you know him and have seen him" (verse 7).

Day Two:

1. Read John 14:8—11.

2. I pray for the grace I want:
   Jesus, help me to know you better
   so that I can love you more
   and follow you more closely.

3. Points:
*(i) "Have I been with you so long, and yet you do not know me?"
(verse 9).*
(ii) "He who has seen me has seen the Father" (verse 9).
*(iii) "Believe me that I am in the Father and the Father is in me"
(verse 11).*

Day Three:

1. Read John 14:12—15.

2. I pray for the grace I want:
   Jesus, help me to know you better
   so that I can love you more
   and follow you more closely.

3. Points:
*(i) "Truly, truly, I say to you, he who believes in me will also do the
works that I do; and greater works that these will he do, because I
go to the Father" (verse 12).*
*(ii) "Whatever you ask in my name, I will do it , that the Father
may be glorified in the Son; if you ask anything in my name, I will
do it" (verses 13—14).*
(iii) "If you love me, you will keep my commandments" (verse 15).

Day Four:

1. Read John 14:16—17.

2. I pray for the grace I want:
   Jesus, help me to know you better
   so that I can love you more
   and follow you more closely.

3. Points:
   (i) "And I will pray the Father, and he will give you another Counsellor, to be with you forever, even the Spirit of truth" (verses 16—17).
   (ii) " . . . the Spirit of truth whom the world cannot receive, because it neither sees him nor knows him" (verse 17).
   (iii) "You know him, for he dwells with you and will be with you" (verse 17).

Day Five:

1. Read John 14:18—24.

2. I pray for the grace I want:
   Jesus, help me to know you better
   so that I can love you more
   and follow you more closely.

3. Points:
   (i) "I will not leave you desolate; I will come to you" (verse 18).
   (ii) "He who has my commandments and keeps them, he it is who loves me; and he who loves me will be loved by

my Father, and I will love him and manifest myself to him" (verse 21).
(iii) "If anyone loves me, he will keep my word, and my Father will love him, and we will come to him and make our home with him" (verse 23).

Day Six:

1. Read John 14:25—31.

2. I pray for the grace I want:
   Jesus, help me to know you better
   so that I can love you more
   and follow you more closely.

3. Points:
   (i) "The Counsellor, the Holy Spirit, whom the Father will send in my name, he will teach you all things" (verse 25).
   (ii) "Peace I leave with you; my peace I give to you; not as the world gives do I give to you. Let not your hearts be troubled, neither let them be afraid" (verse 27).
   (iii) "I do as the Father has commanded me, so that the world may know that I love the Father" (verse 31).

Day Seven:

1. Read John 15:1—4.

2. I pray for the grace I want:
   Jesus, help me to know you better
   so that I can love you more
   and follow you more closely .

3. Points:
> (i) "I am the true vine, and my Father is the vine-dresser. Every branch of mine that bears no fruit he takes away, and every branch that does bear fruit he prunes, that it may bear more fruit" (verses 1—2).
> (ii) "You are already made clean by the word which I have spoken to you" (verse 3).
> (iii) "Abide in me, and I in you" (verse 4).

Day Eight:

1. Read John 15:5—9.

2. I pray for the grace I want:
> Jesus, help me to know you better
> so that I can love you more
> and follow you more closely.

3. Points:
> (i) "I am the vine, you are the branches. He who abides in me, and I in him, he it is that bears much fruit, for apart from me you can do nothing" (verse 5).
> (ii) "If you abide in me, and my words abide in you, ask whatever you will, and it shall be done for you" (verse 7).
> (iii) "As the Father has loved me, so have I loved you; abide in my love" (verse 9).

Day Nine:

1. Read John 15:10—12.

2. I pray for the grace I want:
   Jesus, help me to know you better
   so that I can love you more
   and follow you more closely.

3. Points:
   (i) "If you keep my commandments, you will abide in my love, just as I have kept my Father's Commandments and abide in his love" (verse 10).
   (ii) "These things I have spoken to you, that my joy may be in you, and that your joy may be full" (verse 11).
   (iii) "This is my commandment, that you love one another as I have loved you" (verse 12).

Day Ten:

1. Read John 15:13—15.

2. I pray for the grace I want:
   Jesus, help me to know you better
   so that I can love you more
   and follow you more closely.

3. Points:
   (i) "Greater love has no man that this, that a man lay down his life for his friends" (verse 13).
   (ii) "You are my friends if you do what I command you" (verse 14).

(iii) "No longer do I call you servants, for the servant does not know what his master is doing; but I have called you friends, for all that I have heard from my Father I have made known to you" (verse 15).

Day Eleven:

1. Read John 15:16—27

2. I pray for the grace I want:
   Jesus, help me to know you better
   so that I can love you more
   and follow you more closely.

3. Points:
   (i) "You did not choose me, but I chose you and appointed you that you should go and bear fruit and that your fruit should abide" (verse 16).
   (ii) "Because I chose you out of the world, therefore the world hates you. Remember the word that I said to you, 'A servant is not greater than his master'" (verses 19—20).
   (iii) "You also are witnesses" (verse 27).

Day Twelve:

1. Read John 16:8—11.

2. I pray for the grace I want:
   Jesus, help me to know you better
   so that I can love you more
   and follow you more closely.

3. Points:
   (i) "When the Counsellor comes, he will convince the world of sin and of righteousness and of judgment: of sin, because they do not believe in me" (verses 8—9).
   (ii) "...of righteousness, because I go to the Father" (verse 10).
   (iii) "...of judgment, because the ruler of this world is judged" (verse 11).

Day Thirteen:

1. Read John 16:12—15.

2. I pray for the grace I want;
   Jesus, help me to know you better
   so that I can love you more
   and follow you more closely.

3. Points:
   (i) "When the Spirit of truth comes, he will guide you into all the truth; for he will not speak on his own authority, but whatever he hears he will speak, and he will declare to you the things that are to come" (verse 13).
   (ii) "He will glorify me, for he will take what is mine and declare it to you" (verse 14).
   (iii) "All that the Father has is mine; therefore I said that he will take what is mine and declare it to you" (verse 15).

Day Fourteen:

1. Read John 16:16—24.

2. I pray for the grace I want:
   Jesus, help me to know you better
   so that I can love you more
   and follow you more closely.

3. Points:
   (i) "Truly, truly, I say to you, you will weep and lament, but the world will rejoice; you will be sorrowful, but your sorrow will turn into joy. When a woman is in travail she has sorrow, because her hour has come; but when she is delivered of the child, she no longer remembers the anguish, for joy that a child is born into the world" (verses 20—21).
   (ii) "So you have sorrow now, but I will see you again and your hearts will rejoice, and no one will take your joy from you" (verse 22).
   (iii) "Hitherto you have asked nothing in my name; ask, and you will receive, that your joy may be full" (verse 24).

Day Fifteen:

1. Read John 16:25—28.

2. I pray for the grace I want:
   Jesus, help me to know you better
   so that I can love you more
   and follow you more closely.

3. Points:
   (i) "The hour is coming when I shall no longer speak to you in figures, but tell you plainly of the Father" (verse 25).

(ii) "The Father himself loves you, because you have loved me and have believed that I came from the Father" (verse 27).
(iii) "I came from the Father and have come into the world; again, I am leaving the world and going to the Father" (verse 28).

Day Sixteen:

1. Read John 16:29—33.

2. I pray for the grace I want:
   Jesus, help me to know you better
   so that I can love you more
   and follow you more closely.

3. Points:
   (i) "His disciples said, 'Now we know that you know all things, and need none to question you; by this we believe that you came from God" (verse 30).
   (ii) "I have said this to you, that in me you may have peace" (verse 33).
   (iii) "In the world you will have tribulation; but be of good cheer, I have overcome the world" (verse 33).

Day Seventeen:

1. Read John 17:1—5.

2. I pray for the grace I want:
   Jesus, help me to know you better
   so that I can love you more
   and follow you more closely.

3. Points:
> (i) "Father, the hour has come; glorify your Son that the Son may glorify you, since you have given him power over all flesh, to give eternal life to all whom you have given him" (verses 1—2.
>
> (ii) "This is eternal life, that they know you, the only true God, and Jesus Christ whom you have sent" (verse 3).
>
> (iii) "And now, Father, glorify me in your own presence with the glory that I had with you before the world was made" (verse 5).

Day Eighteen:

1. Read John 17:6—16, Jesus' prayer for his disciples.

2. I pray for the grace I want:
> Jesus, help me to know you better
> so that I can love you more
> and follow you more closely.

3. Points:
> (i) "I am praying for them; I am not praying for the world but for those whom you have given me, for they are yours" Verse 9).
>
> (ii) "All things are yours, and yours are mine, and I am glorified in them" (verse 10).
>
> (iii) "I do not pray that you should take them out of the world, but that you should keep them from the evil one. They are not of the world, even as I am not of the world" (verse 15—16).

Day Nineteen:

1. Read John 17:17—19.

2. I pray for the grace I want:
   Jesus, help me to know you better
   so that I can love you more
   and follow you more closely.

3. Points:
   (i) "Sanctify them in the truth; your word is truth" (verse 17).
   (ii) "As you sent me into the world, so I have sent them into the world" (verse 18).
   (iii) "And for their sake I consecrate myself, that they may also be consecrated in truth" (verse 19).

Day Twenty:

1. Read John 17:20—26.

2. I pray for the grace I want:
   Jesus, help me to know you better
   so that I can love you more
   and follow you more closely.

3. Points:
   (i) "I do not pray for these only, but also for those who believe in me through their word, that they may all be one; even as you, Father, are in me, and I in you, that they also may be in us, so that the world may believe that you have sent me" (verses 20—21).
   (ii) "O righteous Father, the world has not known you,

but I have known you; and these know that you have sent me" (verse 15).

(iii) "I have made known to them you name, and I will make it known, that the love with which you have loved me may be in them, and I in them" (verse 26).

Day Twenty-One:

1. Read John 18:1—11.

2. I pray for the grace that I want when praying about Jesus' suffering and death:

Jesus, help me to know you better
in your suffering,
to have greater love and
compassion for you,
and to enter into your inner
feelings and sufferings.

3. Points:

(i) "Jesus, knowing all that was to befall him, came forward and said to them, 'Whom do you seek?' They answered him, 'Jesus of Nazareth.' Jesus said to them, 'I am he'" (verses 4—5).

(ii) "'If you seek me, let these men go.' This was to fulfill the word which he had spoken, 'Of those whom you have me I lost not one'" (verses 8—9).

(iii) "Jesus said to Peter, 'Put your sword into its sheath; shall I not drink the cup which the Father has given me?'" (verse 11).

Day Twenty-Two:

1. Read John 18:12—27.

2. I pray for the grace I want:
   Jesus, help me to know you better
   in your suffering,
   to have greater love and compassion for you,
   and to enter into your inner feelings and sufferings.

3. Points:
   (i) "The band of soldiers and their captain and the officers of the Jews seized Jesus and bound him. First they led
   him to Annas" (verses 12—13).
   (ii) "Jesus answered him, 'I have spoken openly to the
   world; I have always taught in synagogues and in the
   temple . . . . If I have spoken wrongly, bear witness to the
   wrong; but if I have spoken rightly, why do you strike
   me?'" (verses 20—23.
   (iii) "A kinsman of the man whose ear Peter had cut off
   asked, 'Did I not see you in the garden with him?' Peter
   again denied it, and at once the cock crowed"
   (verses 26—27).

Day Twenty-Three:

1. Read John 18:28—40, Jesus before Pilate.

2. I pray for the grace I want:
   Jesus, help me to know you better
   in your suffering,
   to have greater love and compassion for you,
   and to enter in to your inner feelings and sufferings.

3. Points:

(i) "Jesus answered, 'My kingship is not of this world'" (verse 36).

(ii) "Pilate said to him, 'So you are a king?' Jesus answered, 'You say that I am a king. For this was I born and for this I have come into the world, to bear witness to the truth'" (verse 37).

(iii) "They cried out again, 'Not this man, but Barbabbas!'" (verse 40).

Day Twenty-Four:

1. Read John 19:1—5.

2. I pray for the grace I want:
Jesus, help me to know you better
in your suffering,
to have greater love and compassion for you,
and to enter into your inner feelings and sufferings.

3. Points:

(i) "Then Pilate took Jesus and scourged him" (verse 1).

(ii) "And the soldiers plaited a crown of thorns, and put it on his head, and arrayed him in a purple robe; they came up to him, saying, 'Hail, King of the Jews!' and struck him with their hands" (verses 2—3).

(iii) "Jesus came out, wearing the crown of thorns and the purple robe. Pilate said to them, 'Here is the man!'" (verse 5).

Day Twenty-Five:

1. Read John 19:6—16.

2. I pray for the grace I want:
   Jesus, help me to know you better
   in your suffering,
   to have greater love and compassion for you,
   and to enter into your inner feelings and sufferings.

3. Points:
   (i) "When the chief priests and the officers saw him, they cried out, 'Crucify him, crucify him!'" (verse 6).
   (ii) "Jesus answered Pilate, 'You would have no power over me unless it had been given you from above'" (verse 11).
   (iii) "Pilate said to the Jews, 'Here is your King!' They cried out, 'Away with him, away with him, crucify him!' Pilate said to them, 'Shall I crucify your King?' The chief priests answered, 'We have no king but Caesar.' Then he handed him over to them to be crucified" (verses 14—160).

Day Twenty-Six:

1. Read John 19:17—22.

2. I pray for the grace I want:
   Jesus, help me to know you better
   in your suffering,
   to have greater love and compassion for you,
   and to enter into your inner feelings and sufferings.

3. Points:

(i) "They took Jesus, and he went out, bearing his own cross" (verse 17).

(ii) "They crucified him" (verse 18).

(iii) "Pilate also wrote a title and put it on the cross; it read, 'Jesus of Nazareth, the King of the Jews'" (verse 19).

Day Twenty-Seven:

1. Read John 19:23—27.

2. I pray for the grace I want:
Jesus, help me to know you better
in your suffering,
to have greater love and compassion for you,
and to enter into your inner feelings and sufferings.

3. Points:

(i) "Standing by the cross were his mother, and his mother's sister, Mary the wife of Clopas, and Mary Magdalene" (verse 25).

(ii) "When Jesus saw his mother, and the disciple whom he loved standing near, he said to his mother, 'Woman, behold your son!' Then he said to the disciple, 'Behold, your mother!'" (verses 26—27).

(iii) "And from that hour the disciple took her to his own house" (verse 27).

Day Twenty-Eight:

1. Read John 19:28—37.

2. I pray for the grace I want:
Jesus, help me to know you better
in your suffering,
to have greater love and compassion for you,
and to enter into your inner feelings and sufferings.

3. Points:
(i) "Jesus said, 'I thirst'" (verse 28).
(ii) "When Jesus had received the vinegar, he said, 'It is finished'; he bowed his head and gave up his spirit" (verse 30).
(iii) "One of the soldiers pierced his side with a spear, and at once there came out blood and water" (verse 34).

Day Twenty-Nine:

1. Read John 20:1—18.

2. I pray for the grace that I want when praying about Jesus' resurrection and his resurrection appearances:
Jesus, help me to know you better
and to enter into the joy and gladness
of your resurrection,
so that I can love you more
and follow you more closely.

3. Points:
(i) "Mary Magdalene came to the tomb early, while it was still dark, and saw that the stone had been taken way from the tomb" (verse 1).
(ii) "She turned round and saw Jesus standing, but she did not know that it was Jesus. Jesus said to her, 'Woman, why are you weeping? Whom do you seek?' Supposing him to be the gardener, she said to him, 'Sir, if you have carried

him away, tell me where you have laid him, and I will take him away.' Jesus said to her, 'Mary.' She turned and said to him, 'Rabboni' (which means Teacher)" (verses 14—16). (iii) "Mary Magdalene went and said to the disciples, 'I have seen the Lord'; and she told them that he had said these things to her" (verse 18).

Day Thirty:

1. Read John 20:19—23.

2. I pray for the grace I want:
   Jesus, help me to know you better
   and to enter into the joy and gladness
   of your resurrection,
   so that I can love you more
   and follow you more closely.

3. Points:
   (i) "On the evening of that day, the first day of the week, the doors being shut where the disciples were, for fear of the Jews, Jesus came and stood among them and said, 'Peace be with you'" (verse 19).
   (ii) "He showed them his hands and his side. The disciples were glad when they saw the Lord" (verse 20).
   (iii) "'As the Father has sent me, so I send you.' And when he had said this, he breathed on them, and said to them, 'Receive the Holy Spirit. If you forgive the sins of any, they are forgiven; if you retain the sins of any, they are retained'" (verses 22—23).

Day Thirty-One:

1. Read John 20:24—31.

2. I pray for the grace I want:
   Jesus, help me to know you better
   and to enter into the joy and gladness
   of your resurrection,
   so that I can love you more
   and follow you more closely.

3. Points:
   (i) "Thomas was with them. The doors were shut, but Jesus came and stood among them, and said, 'Peace be with you'" (verse 26).
   (ii) "He said to Thomas, 'Put your finger here, and see my hands; and put out your hand, and place it in my side; do not be faithless, but believing.' Thomas answered him, 'My Lord and my God!'" (verses 27—28).
   (iii) "Jesus said to him, 'Have you believe because you have seen me? Blessed are those who have not seen and yet believe.'" (verse 29).

Day Thirty-Two:

1. Read John 20:30—31.

2. I pray for the grace I want:
   Jesus, help me to know you better
   and to enter into the joy and gladness
   of your resurrection,
   so that I can love you more
   and follow you more closely.

3. Points:

(i) "Jesus did many other signs in the presence of the disciples, which are not written in this book" (verse 30).
(ii) "These are written that you may believe that Jesus is the Christ, the Son of God . . ." (verse 31).
(iii) " . . . and that believing you may have life in his name" (verse 31).

Day Thirty-Three:

1. Read John 21:1—8.

2. I pray for the grace I want:
   Jesus, help me to know you better
   and to enter into the joy and gladness
   of your resurrection,
   so that I can love you more
   and follow you more closely.

3. Points:
   (i) "Just as the day was breaking, Jesus stood on the beach; yet the disciples did not know that it was Jesus" (verse 4).
   (ii) "He said to them, 'Cast the net on the right side of the boat. . . . ' So they cast it, and now they were not able to haul it in, for the quantity of fish" (verse 6).
   (iii) "That disciple whom Jesus loved said to Peter, 'It is the Lord'" (verse 7).

Day Thirty-Four:

1. Read John 21:9—14.

2. I pray for the grace I want:
   Jesus, help me to know you better
   and to enter into the joy and gladness
   of your resurrection,
   so that I can love you more
   and follow you more closely.

3. Points:
   (i) "Jesus said to them, 'Come and have breakfast'"
   (verse 12).
   (ii) "None of the disciples dared ask him, 'Who are you?'
   They knew it was the Lord" (verse 13).
   (iii) "Jesus came and took the bread and gave it to them,
   and so with the fish" (verse 14).

Day Thirty-Five:

1. Read John 21:15—23.

2. I pray for the grace I want:
   Jesus, help me to know you better
   and to enter into the joy and gladness
   of your resurrection,
   so that I can love you more
   and follow you more closely.

3. Points:
   (i) "Jesus said to Simon Peter, 'Simon, son of John, do you
   love me more that these?' He said to him, 'Yes , Lord, you
   know that I love you.' He said to him, 'Feed my lambs'"

(verse 15).

(ii) "A second time he said to him, 'Simon, son of John, do you love me?' He said to him, 'Yes, Lord, you know that I love you.' He said to him, 'Tend my sheep'" (verse 16).

(iii) "He said to him the third time, 'Simon, son of John, do you love me?' ...And he said to him, 'Lord, you know everything; you know that I love you.' Jesus said to him, 'Feed my sheep.' ...And after this he said to him, 'Follow me'" (verses 17—19).